PAST IMPERFECT

Published by Novel Novella Publishing

Copyright © 2022 G D Harrison

All rights reserved
G D Harrison has asserted his right
under the Copyright, Designs and Patents Act 1988
to be identified as the author of this work
ISBN 978-1-84396-671-5

Also available as a Kindle ebook
ISBN 978-1-84396-626-5

A catalogue record for this book is available from the British Library and the American Library of Congress.

This is a work of fiction. Any resemblance between the characters and situations depicted and those in real life is purely coincidental.

No part of this book may be reproduced in any material or electronic form, including photocopying, without written permission from the publisher, except for the quotation of brief passages in criticism.

Typesetting and pre-press production
eBook Versions
27 Old Gloucester Street
London WC1N 3AX
www.ebookversions.com

PAST IMPERFECT

G D Harrison

Novel Novella Publishing

Contents

1
Chapter One
Samuel

4
Chapter Two
Parenting

9
Chapter Three
The Visit

20
Chapter Four
Travelling Back in Time

33
Chapter Five
Progress

41
Chapter Six
Long Distance, Long Memory

52
Chapter Seven
Blue Car Blues

62
Chapter Eight
Hidden Gems

75
Chapter Nine
Return of the Jack

99
Chapter Ten
Return of the Colin

126
Chapter Eleven
Old Memories, New Beginnings

136
Chapter Twelve
A Picture Paints a Thousand Memories

141
Chapter Thirteen
Past Imperfect

156
Chapter Fourteen
Hello Old F(r)iend

169
Chapter Fifteen
Past, I'm Perfect

CHAPTER ONE
Samuel

I'm Samuel.

I am twelve years old.

I live with my mother and father.

I go to school and like collecting stamps and playing conkers. I like cricket too. I don't like girls; girls are silly and don't like boy's things. I am not at school at the moment 'cos it's the holidays and we don't go to school during the holidays; we stay at home or go out for the day instead. But I think I may have broken my leg playing cricket as I don't go out much now.

My mother and father get angry with me. They don't understand me and I don't understand what they are telling me. My friends, Bill and Michael, understand me and I understand them. Why can't my mother and father be like them?

My mother shouts at me sometimes; it frightens me and I often cry. She takes pills to make her feel better and then she hugs me. I like hugs and cuddles as it stops me from being afraid of her shouting at me. She cries sometimes too.

My father is calmer, but he isn't often at home as he works late sometimes, and I'm always asleep when he gets back from work. He goes to work before I am awake too. I see him on Saturdays and Sundays but I don't think he likes me 'cos he doesn't give me hugs and cuddles. But he doesn't shout at me much either. Perhaps he's not my father. Bill says that boys sometimes have more than one father…or mother. Bill says that sometimes mothers and fathers don't live with each other and another mother or father comes along to stay instead. But I think my mother and father have been with me my whole life, so perhaps my father just doesn't love me.

Michael doesn't have a father. His father died in a war. He has a mother but she is always miserable. But I don't think that she shouts at him. She does give him lots of hugs. I think my mother gives me more hugs than Michael's mother gives him. But my mother shouts more at me. Perhaps she has to shout to give me a hug. She throws things too. She threw a picture on the floor. The glass broke. It was a photograph of a man; I don't know who it was, but she got even more upset when the picture got broken.

Sometimes I don't eat her dinners; I'm just not hungry. She gets angry and shouts at me and she leaves the dinner with me in the bedroom, saying that I am not getting anything else until I've eaten up what she's already made me. It stays there all night sometimes and is still there in the morning when I wake up.

I know there are other rooms in the house but I never seem to go into them. I just don't feel like doing so. I don't want to go into the other bedrooms. I like it here in this one.

I sit up and look out of the window and look at the cars. I like cars; I like blue cars best of all. Uncle Jack had a blue car. I think it was a Ford.

A man came to visit. He had a blue Ford. I thought it might be Uncle Jack but it didn't look like Uncle Jack and he didn't take me out, so it couldn't have been him. But he had a blue

Ford.

He visited me several times and he did say that he had bought Uncle Jack's car, which is why I recognised it, although it looked different; perhaps he had cleaned it.

I only wanted to talk about Uncle Jack and when he would take me out again. I had hoped that this new man would take me out in Uncle Jack's car but he never asked me and I didn't ask him.

The man stopped coming to see me for a while; I don't know how long he didn't visit me, but I just kept expecting him and he didn't come to see me when I thought he would. At least I think he was going to see me again. But then Uncle Jack came back and I think he played some music to me.

Sometimes I can't remember what I've forgotten…

CHAPTER TWO
Parenting

Josie and Steve sat in the front room of their semi-detached house. They were watching the evening television. The house was in an established street, in what had been a market town but which over the decades had been forced to adopt a different existence; it was now a commuter town with a burgeoning population of the travelling class. Whatever history had developed in the town had been squeezed into the corners of libraries and into the failing memories of its older residents, as new shops replaced traditional family run businesses and new residents replaced those that either moved away, or who retreated to their photo albums containing images of earlier times.

There was nothing special about the house; it was like all the rest in the street. Maybe the odd neighbour had put an extra room in the loft, or converted the garage into an additional living space, but apart from the desire to expand into whatever footprint the dwelling already had, nothing much had changed since the properties were originally built back at the turn of the previous century. Most changes were therefore cosmetic; a new kitchen or bathroom, a different colour scheme or a conservatory. This wasn't an area where the houses were substantial in size that warranted the option of conversion into a block of flats; all the properties were restricted to their original two or three bedrooms. This was the status of Josie and Steve's house. It was basically as they had found it but with the addition of personal touches to make it their own.

Josie was in her thirties, slim, petite with brown eyes and a similar shade of hair. Steve was of a similar age but a more burley fellow, and in some lights probably looked twice her size. He wasn't obese, but as an ex-rugby player he had a degree of bulk about him, and with fair hair and blue eyes, the pair obviously fitted into the category of 'opposites attract'.

This evening was like most evenings; Steve would laugh at regular intervals, spurred on by the fabricated laughter of the sitcom that they were watching. Josie didn't know whether Steve genuinely found the programme amusing, or whether he was just being coerced into enjoying the programme by the canned response of the supposed 'live' audience. She wasn't laughing. She had a topic that she needed to discuss with Steve but she wanted to choose the correct moment, so that Steve would engage properly with her, rather than him just agreeing with everything she said for an easy life.

She looked at the clock on the wall. The television programme would finish shortly. Then it would be the news, which Steve had already watched on one of the other channels an hour earlier. Nothing could have happened in the intervening period, so she chose the break at the top of the hour as her moment to start the conversation:

"He didn't eat his dinner again today," she said, with a resigned air of defeat.

Steve didn't respond verbally but just glanced across at his wife with a similar air of acceptance of the situation that Josie had described. He chose not to add anything as he could see that she had further words ready to be propelled in his direction.

"I know he's not going to get any better. I know that, but I just wish that he would respond now and again to what I am saying. I know the doctor said that he won't understand everything we say but why can't he understand something rather than nothing?"

At this point she broke down and started to sob uncontrollably. Steve knew that this was his cue to move out of his chair and join her on the sofa. He duly obliged and put his arm around her in a comforting manner and tried to ease the situation with some words of solace:

"I know, I know. It's very frustrating for both of us but I can't see that we can do anymore ourselves. You love him dearly and I am sure that he knows that," said Steve.

Josie responded by jerking her body and throwing Steve's arm away from her. It was evident that she had noticed that Steve had only referred to her loving him and did not include himself in that love.

"You're never bloody here to experience my day with him! It's impossible to see somebody you love just…he can't hold a conversation with me; he doesn't even understand me! He just sits there with this dead look in his eyes. He doesn't even look at me!"

Josie couldn't continue any more with her feelings and again sobbed uncontrollably. Steve was hesitant but again put his arm around his wife to comfort her. She didn't resist but continued to cry and breathe in an erratic fashion.

Steve said something that had been in his mind for several

months:

"Why don't we get help? I don't mean move him into a home somewhere, but why can't we have somebody come around and take the strain off of us with some professional help?"

Steve's comments were well meant but Josie snapped:

"What do you mean, 'our strain' – you are never bloody here! You go to work before he is awake, you spend all day away from the problem, come back after he has gone to sleep and eat your dinner and watch bloody TV! That's all you do. You probably can't remember what he even looks like!"

Steve glanced across at the array of photographs, which were neatly framed on the sideboard, and picked out the one of Sam. It wasn't that he had forgotten what Sam looked like; it was an involuntary action that resulted from Josie's rant.

"I know, I know," he said, still trying to comfort her, "let's get some help." Between the sobs Josie nodded. She had reached her end.

The following day Steve returned from work to declare that he had arranged for a social worker to visit from a specialised unit. They would phone Josie during the week to arrange a convenient time for an initial assessment visit. Steve didn't elaborate with Josie as to what would happen and what was expected, primarily because he hadn't elaborated during the conversation that he had had with Social Services. He thought it would be best for history to take its natural course.

Josie had been reluctant to involve any outside help and Steve didn't think it was worthwhile confusing the situation by adding information that may be inaccurate. As Josie had said, he was never at home to witness events. This did at least place a muted smile on Josie's face. It was almost a reluctant one, but it hid her appreciation that Steve had finally joined in with what she was facing every day. Of course, he wouldn't be around when the visits took place but he had nevertheless done something. She was secretly pleased and hugged him with gratification.

Steve felt the appreciation in her grip and wondered whether he should have been more proactive earlier, but it had always been Josie who had resisted any outside help, and if he had approached the subject at the wrong time, or during the wrong occasion, then perhaps they would be further away from a conclusion than they already were. Steve convinced himself that he had done the right thing.

That evening Steve decided to eat his evening meal on the sofa and sat next to Josie. Josie was obviously surprised and didn't say anything but shifted over to make more room for her new companion. She realised that Steve was trying to align himself with her, as tensions had always been high in the house, and perhaps him taking control of the visits had been duly recognised. Previously Josie would have ushered him back to his own chair. Things were improving.

CHAPTER THREE
The Visit

Colin Smith knocked on the door and awaited a response from inside. He was a tall, slim man, probably in his late forties or early fifties, casually dressed but at the same time conveyed an air of authority. He was blessed with a full set of dark brown hair and kind dark brown eyes that were of a similar hue. He had a blue and white lanyard around his neck, which had an identification photo with his name and other details encased in a transparent, laminated, rectangular holder. The photo must have been taken several years ago, as whilst the image definitely matched the person that was attached to it, the face looked younger. Not younger as in a school photo, but rather that there weren't quite as many experience lines etched on the face. Either that or the equipment used to take the photo wasn't of today's UHD standard.

The door opened and Colin smiled, held out his hand with his ID card and positioned it in front of the occupier.

"Hi, I'm Colin Smith from the local Health Authority Support Team. You must be Josie."

It was indeed Josie who answered the door, and there was a look of relief on her face that implied that she had just been rescued from a burning building. She hoped that she didn't appear too desperate.

She had been fearful that her visitor may have been too large to fit into Steve's armchair, so she had been quite prepared to vacate her normal sofa position to allow him a more comfortable perch, but he appeared to be only slightly wider than her, although considerably taller. His hair was a similar shade. Neither seemed to have enhanced their appearance with a hair dye, and whilst Mr Smith was about two decades older, his dark brown eyes eluded to a similar hue to her own. She felt an instant rapport with whom she hoped would be her saviour.

"Come in," she said, and led Colin into the front room of the house, beckoning him to sit in the armchair that had been neatly arranged so that it faced the two-seater sofa rather than the television, which was its normal alignment.

"Can I get you a tea or coffee?" she said, in a manner that she thought Colin had heard a thousand times before. He had, and he responded as he always did: "Coffee, white, no sugar would be lovely!"

He wasn't really thirsty, however the offer and acceptance of a coffee always set a relaxed atmosphere. It also gave him the chance to take a general overview of the family's lifestyle whilst the host was out of the room. He also wasn't really a lover of coffee; tea was his favoured drink but coffee was an easier hot drink to produce, and he always thought it best to ask his host for something that was simple to prepare. Tea always required the host to stay in the kitchen for several minutes whilst the concoction brewed, whereas coffee was a quick boil, spoonful of coffee, milk and stir. The time it would take for the production of a cup of tea meant that there was always either an embarrassing silence, or a shouting exchange between Colin and wherever the kitchen was. Tea was what he had been weaned on, and apart from the surprisingly excellent coffee which was available from the café across the road from his office at work, these visits were the only occasion when he agreed to its supply.

He glanced around and noticed a series of photos in frames that were neatly arranged on the sideboard to his right. He studied the occupants as best he could from his position. His attention was immediately drawn to a wooden framed photograph of a man. The glass was broken but all the pieces were still in their correct place. The photograph was a head and shoulders image of a man in his fifties or sixties who was smiling, as if he had just been told a joke and the camera had caught his reaction at just the right moment. He was smartly dressed in a suit jacket and tie. Colin surmised that the photo was taken at a family celebration; perhaps a wedding or some other form of anniversary. There were other photos in frames. All were either of people or animals, and each was in a near identical wooden frame, which complimented the sideboard that they were carefully arranged upon. This conveyed a degree of order about the household.

Colin turned to position himself towards the opposite side of the room. He noticed a large flat screen television that was neatly arranged at an angle on top of a console, which also housed a satellite receiver and some DVDs. He noticed one that stood out from the rest. It was white and had the words 'Our Wedding' carefully written on the spine.

His thoughts were interrupted by a voice from the back of the house.

"You did say no sugar, didn't you?" It was Josie just

confirming his request.

"Yes," he replied, and with that confirmation Josie entered the room, carefully carrying a mug in each hand.

"There you are," she said, as she carefully placed both items on pre-arranged coasters, which were located on top of a small table that lay in front of the sofa, but which was within easy reach of Colin's seat. He smiled in acceptance and waited for Josie to volunteer her story. He didn't have to wait long.

"Thank you for coming to see us today," she said, "I am really grateful for you fitting us into your schedule."

Colin had heard this sort of opening before. It was usually volunteered by people who had held out for as long as they could, but eventually accepted the inevitable and had asked for help. Colin thought that this was because they felt guilty at not being able to cope with what was a personal family matter. It was a defeat in their eyes, as if they had failed in some way to cope with a loved one's problems. He tried to start by confronting that mind-set.

"I have to say that you should in no way feel defeated; you have coped admirably well in very difficult circumstances, and I am amazed that you have waited so long to ask for our help. You should applaud yourself."

Josie nodded appreciatively but Colin could see that she was holding back emotions that were very near the surface.

"Tell me, why have you kept Sam here for so long?" He carefully looked down at his notes to check that he had the name correct.

"It's where he grew up. It's the only house he has ever lived in and I thought that if we moved him out to somewhere else, then that would upset him…upset his routine and make him worse. I think all the time we were stupidly thinking that he could get better and recover but all I have done is perhaps prolong the agony."

At this point Josie started to well up and Colin wasn't sure whether the agony had been prolonged for Sam or for Josie and her husband, but it was a similar story that he had heard many times.

Colin tried to offer well-rehearsed words of comfort:

"Now, you have done a sterling job and I am sure that Sam does like being in familiar surroundings. That has got to be beneficial; it usually is. Wouldn't you be happier in familiar surroundings if you were seriously unwell?"

Josie couldn't answer but nodded and gave a slight smile in acknowledgement. Colin continued:

"I don't usually meet with the patient on this visit but I would just like to get a story from you about Sam, so that I can bring snippets into any future conversation with him. It sometimes helps to unlock some memories. Sometimes we can get a conversation going. So, tell me a bit about him."

Josie gathered her composure and slowly wiped her eyes and nose with a patterned hankie that she had pulled from her skirt pocket.

"Well, he's been on a downward spiral for some time. He had a great love of cricket and used to play for the local team. He got hit on the head several years ago, and looking back we wonder if that had anything to do with his current condition. When he occasionally engages with me, he talks about a Bill and Michael but we don't know who they are; maybe they were in the cricket team."

Colin nodded, and by now he had opened up his notebook

to the next page and was scribbling away in his own form of shorthand; basically, elongated scribble that he would guess at later on. Josie continued:

"Apart from the odd word he doesn't really say or do anything. He really is in a different world to us and I must admit that I do lose my temper and shout at him in frustration – sometimes I just can't take it. It's impossible sometimes to cope." Josie broke down again and Colin did his usual, 'there, there', which seemed to cure all ills, and Josie eventually continued:

"If I could know what he is thinking, then I could perhaps interact with him, but I don't even know if he knows what I am saying. That is what is so frustrating; the inability to talk to him properly."

Colin felt that it was his turn.

"Okay, you've done extremely well and it is my job to see if we can help you and Sam cope with his condition; make you both as happy as possible with his remaining days." Colin wanted to say 'remaining years' but both he and Josie realised that years were probably out of the question. Days seemed appropriate but somehow more final.

The conversation was interrupted by the opening of the front door and the unexpected vision of Steve entering the house. Josie stared in surprise; it wasn't 'home' time.

"Hi all, sorry I'm late but had trouble with the trains," said Steve. "What are you doing here?" asked a surprised Josie.

"When I made the initial call to these guys, it was suggested that we were both here. So here I am!" Josie smiled in a manner that her face hadn't seen in many a year. Steve was at last showing support.

Colin acknowledged Steve's arrival and waited for him to

settle down next to his wife on the settee. He then continued with his thoughts:

"Your frustration sometimes boils over and you then feel guilty, don't you?" His question was directed at both of them but it was pretty obvious that he was meaning this to be answered by Josie.

"Yes," she replied, and glanced towards the sideboard and the collection of photographs.

"I had this photo in my hand the other day and I took it up to dad to see if I could get a spark of recognition out of him; whether he could recognise the picture. He just stared at it blankly."

Josie moved over to the sideboard and picked up the photograph with the broken glass and volunteered it to Colin. Colin accepted the movement and held the wooden frame in his left hand. He studied it in greater detail than he had done when he had first sat down. The picture showed a happy chap with bright eyes and a kind nature that flooded out of the photograph and towards the viewer.

"He looks really happy," said Colin.

"Yes, that's why I showed it to him. It was taken at our wedding and he had a lovely time. I had hoped that he would have remembered that the occasion was our wedding - but nothing; just a blank, gaunt stare that is so upsetting."

"I can well imagine just how upsetting that would be," continued Colin, "it is meant to be the happiest day of your life and you want him to still be part of it. Perhaps it would help if I explain what is probably going on."

Josie reached out to Colin for the return of the picture, and on retrieving it, held it tight to her chest in anticipation of squeezing the last bit of love out of the photograph.

Colin continued:

"It's like this, he hasn't forgotten anything. In his world your wedding hasn't happened yet. His mind contains only events that he has amassed up to his 'brain age'. Whilst his capacity to remember what you want him to remember is not there, his mind contains only events that have happened to him up to a certain point in his life. It's not crammed with every job interview, girlfriend, football match he has viewed, or Christmas celebration that his body has experienced. Your wedding doesn't exist yet in his world. That actually gives me an advantage."

Josie and Steve looked at him in unison with surprised expressions meandering across their faces.

"His mind only has a certain number of events recorded; think of it like a series of holiday snaps held on a DVD. You put the disc into the machine and by mistake you delete some of the pictures. All the images were there but now you can only recall a certain percentage; the rest have gone, and whilst you know that they were once there, anybody else who is unfamiliar with the pictures on the disc, only sees what remains. To them, the lost images never existed. That's the situation your dad finds himself in. But what that means is that the images that remain should be more memorable; there are less images to remember and therefore each should be more readily available for recall."

Colin moved over to the book case that was adjacent to the TV unit and carefully selected a book on wildlife. He quickly took a look inside to check its suitability and then moved over towards his audience. He held the book out towards the pair and flicked through the pages. They revealed a series of wildlife photos that rapidly appeared and disappeared as the pages advanced in quick succession.

"What did you see?" he asked of the couple.

Steve volunteered an answer: "A couple of lions, a giraffe and a hippo," he said.

Josie didn't say anything but just nodded. She felt safer agreeing with her husband than potentially saying the wrong thing and being seen as a fool.

"Okay," said Colin, and he proceeded to repeat the experiment but this time only selected half of the total number of pages. Again, they appeared and disappeared in quick succession as he flicked the pages in front of the pair.

"Right, what did you see this time?" he said.

Again, Steve volunteered his answer: "The lions, the giraffe, some birds, a croc and a monkey or gorilla". He looked pleased with his response and turned to Josie to see if she saw anything different.

Josie felt confident enough to speak: "I saw the lions and the giraffe, the birds, a monkey, a Land Rover, or something similar, and a view of the Savannah."

Colin didn't need to say anything further to prove his point but felt obliged to do so anyway: "So, you both saw more when the potential number of images was reduced." Both nodded.

"But did you actually see more or do you really just remember more?"

The question didn't need an answer and none was forthcoming. Colin just continued with his lecture: "The point is that the less information the brain has stored, the more easily it can be retrieved. Sam can probably remember a higher percentage of facts and images than you or I because he has less clutter in his memory banks. Because he has less info stored, we can ask him a question about something that happened to him in his early years, which he would not be able to recall if his brain age was the same as his body age. However, his brain age is much earlier and will contain less experiences, so there is a better chance of specific info being recalled. Think of it as a form of time travel."

Colin looked towards Josie and Steve, as if asking for permission to continue, or at least to pass some form of comment. After all, time travel is not something that you can do every day. He continued:

"You need to stop getting frustrated with your father. You're in the present but he is probably several decades further back in time, so stop getting all three of you in a state by insisting that he joins you in the now. You need to travel back to where he is. Join him there; he'll be happier because he'll be in familiar surroundings and you'll be less frustrated. Maybe you'll be able to come off of those tranquilizers."

This seemed to take the couple by surprise at the realisation that they had been trying to dictate the terms of any conversation with Sam. Josie also didn't realise that her addiction to her pills was so obvious. Perhaps Colin's suggestion would work.

Josie volunteered a response:

"Okay, so if we ask him general questions about how he is feeling, what he likes doing, who his friends are, what he did yesterday and just roll with the answers…don't correct him and don't give any ground to trying to prove him wrong."

Colin nodded, as if giving permission, and continued with his quest.

"What I would like to do is perhaps work more closely with

Sam. My mother used to live around here and I'd be interested to know if your father can remember what the area was like in those days. It might help if I can engage with him in a meaningful conversation about something he is experiencing in his world, before he loses everything to the progression of his condition. Perhaps I could come around twice a week?"

The pair nodded again, which Colin took as a sign of acceptance of his proposal. He felt that he had concluded the visit and suggested the following Tuesday as a suitable starting point, with Friday being the follow up for the week. All was agreed and there was the usual shaking of hands and pleasantries when somebody leaves a house.

The coffee was untouched and remained on the table. Colin had never really wanted to drink it; he rarely did on such occasions as he viewed it more as part of a greeting, such as 'How are you?'. It was rarely a genuine question, more of a conversation starter to get both parties used to each other.

Josie's life was hopefully going to be easier from here on in, or at least less frustrating.

CHAPTER FOUR
Travelling Back in Time

Tuesday arrived and Colin presented himself at the front door at the agreed time. He didn't need to knock as Josie had been cleaning in the front room and had seen Colin park his blue Ford in the street outside. She hurried to the door to let him in.

"Good Morning!" beamed Colin, who appeared to be way too cheerful for his profession.

He must get involved in some terribly depressing work and Josie wondered if he took anything, to either help him forget or to see him through the day. Perhaps he got blitzed at the weekend.

Josie returned the greeting and asked how he was.

"Fine, fine, thank you. How's our man today?"

Josie didn't really need to say anything as Colin probably knew the answer, but she responded anyway:

"No different to normal. He's upstairs in bed still, I'm afraid. He rarely gets out of bed. He thinks his legs don't work but a doctor has tested him out and can find nothing wrong. We think it may have something to do with when he broke a leg, when he first attended secondary school. I remember him telling me about it when I broke my own leg at a similar age."

"So, he'd be about twelve," interjected Colin.

"Yes, I suppose so. I'd better take you up. He knows you're coming. I told him yesterday, and earlier this morning, but it didn't seem to get him inspired enough to get up to see you. Sorry, you'll have to take him as you find him."

"No worries," replied Colin, and with that remark the two of them ascended the stairs that formed a direct line from the front door.

Josie approached the bedroom, which was at the front of the house, and gently knocked on the door, whilst peering through the gap between it and the frame.

"Dad, Colin Smith is here to see you."

She said this as a warning of their impending entry into his room, which didn't seem to register with Sam, as they found him still in bed with his head facing the window.

"Here's Colin," said Josie.

"Leave us to it," responded Colin, trying to take any potential anguish away from her.

Josie was probably relieved, as she didn't argue with the suggestion and duly smiled and left the two alone.

Colin looked at Sam and tried to pair his face with that in the broken picture downstairs. There was no resemblance and he could easily see why any normal person would not recognise the subject of the photo. Colin sat down on a stool, which was adjacent to the bed and positioned about halfway along its length. He thought that his duty was to break the ice and start the conversation. He wasn't really looking for a reply but was just trying to gauge whether Sam was in a responsive mood at all.

"Hello Sam, I'm Colin, how are you feeling today?"

Sam continued to look out of the window but much to

Colin's surprise volunteered a comment. It wasn't in response to Colin's contrived question but it was a response nevertheless.

"Ford; blue isn't it?" was the opening response in a broken and gravelly voice. Colin was taken aback but was pleased at an engagement so soon in his visit. "Yes. Yes, it's a Ford. Do you like cars?"

This was the question. It opened up a reply that he could never have wished for.

"I like cars. Uncle Jack's got a Ford – did you borrow it from Uncle Jack? …it's blue with shiny bits at the front and back… I went in it once… he took me to the park and to the picture house in it…I had an ice cream; it was strawberry…when we got back it was dark and my mum was cross 'cos Uncle Jack brought me back later than he said he would…I didn't go out much with him again. Are you going to take me out?"

Colin took in all the information. He had experienced this sort of response before but not normally so soon in his visits. He had got used to the nature of any such conversation. To anybody outside of his profession, it must have appeared strange; here was a seventy-something year old man with a permanent gaunt expression in his face, yet speaking like a twelve-year-old about obscure things. All the subject matter was in rapid succession, as if all the information had to be expelled before his breath had gone. Colin didn't really know why; he was just grateful that Sam had engaged with him.

"Did you…I mean, do you like Uncle Jack?" Colin managed to correct himself in time. He almost fell into the trap of separating today from yesteryear.

Sam continued with his tirade:

"He bought me ice cream; it was strawberry…it was pink…

his car was blue with shiny bits at the front and back…mum was cross…I think she sent him away…"

Colin didn't interrupt but let Sam finish and waited for a natural pause before continuing: "Did you get sent to your room?"

"Yes…mum was cross…I didn't have any tea…she said I'd had ice cream and that would have to do…"

With that last series of words, the conversation ended. It was almost as if a quota had been used up. Colin compared it to a fairground mechanical machine into which you'd place a coin, and it would buy you so many seconds or minutes to retrieve a toy, using a claw and joystick. Your money would run out and the machine would just stop. You could put another coin in and start the process again but no matter what Colin said or did, Sam would not respond. Colin had used his money's worth for the day.

Colin took up the remainder of his allotted time by jotting down notes of the conversation and Sam's general demeanour. He would occasionally look up to see if Sam had changed his position, but on each occasion he remained fixed, looking out of the window from his semi-upright position.

Colin's car was the focus of Sam's attention. Colin wondered whether he could open up the conversation by suggesting that he could take Sam out, but without Josie's permission that would be difficult. It might also be unwise and outside of his remit, but it was food for thought and one that he jotted down in his notebook.

When Colin had finished his jottings, he said his goodbye to his now unresponsive client and went downstairs where he was met by Josie, who had surmised that Colin had finished with Sam for the day.

"How did it go? she enquired.

"Well, Sam focused on my car and talked about events surrounding a blue car that he knew of but then he clammed up. Apparently, there was an Uncle Jack that had a similar coloured car to my own and that seemed to unlock the juices; but only so far. Shame, but I got some notes from which to work. Are we still okay for Friday?"

"Yes, of course," replied Josie, who by now had ushered Colin towards the door.

Colin duly opened the front door and exited out into the garden, following the path around the flowerbed and towards his car, which was parked on the street outside. He opened the door, and as he turned to sit in the driver's seat, he took a glance up at Sam's bedroom window. Sam was still staring in his general direction. No expression; no wave good-bye.

Colin turned the key in the ignition, put on his seatbelt and indicated to pull away from the kerb, and with one flowing move he gently edged into the near-empty street. He was in two minds whether to drive around the block to see if Sam was still staring out of the window, but he thought better of it and decided to end his working day there.

About twenty miles later, Colin pulled into the driveway of his house, carefully applied the handbrake and exited the car. He strode purposefully towards the front door and in doing so pressed the 'lock' button on his key fob. There was a satisfying 'beep' that told him all was well behind him but that would be the last piece of good news for the day. He carefully inserted his door key into its rightful place, turned the handle and entered the house and with a cheery disposition said:

"Mumsie, I'm home!"

There was a sobbing from the front room. Colin immediately put down his jotter book onto a small table that lay inside by the front door, and nudged the door closed with the sole of his right shoe.

"What's wrong Mumsie?" he asked.

'Mumsie' was a woman in her seventies, who sat semi-crouched on the settee. She was holding a handkerchief close to her face. She was normally an upright, semi-cheerful person, who had been through a lot in her lifetime but who had somehow managed to look reasonably youthful for her age. Her hair was an aged grey but was full of volume. In her youth it had been a natural deep brown and the style hadn't changed much during the intervening years, so her overall appearance had just faded over time. Her past and her present were easily matched.

"I'm sorry…" she said with an apologetic voice, "…but your cousin has sent me through this family tree that she has been doing and it's opened up a few old wounds."

The words sounded rehearsed and Colin wondered how long his mother had been preparing them. He also thought that he knew what the old wounds were. From an early age he had been told that his father had been killed whilst on a naval exercise. In fact, he never knew his father at all and had only seen a few photographs of him that his mother had positioned around the house. He had spent his whole life without a father and it was apparent that he could cope with the loss far better than his mother, who was obviously finding it difficult, even numerous decades later.

"There, there…we're alright Mumsie!" said Colin in a

cheerful voice, trying desperately to bring his mother back to normality but she kept sobbing. It wasn't an uncontrollable sob, more of a hesitant, erratic breathing that was interspersed with a watering of the eyes. Colin couldn't tell whether she had been holding back the tears and his arrival had opened the sluice gates, or whether she had been crying constantly since she had received the information. Eventually she calmed herself and nervously showed Colin the family tree.

The tree had been expertly drawn in freehand and resembled a large oak bereft of its foliage. The branches were formed of names and dates, and at first glance it was all rather confusing to the eye, but gradually Colin focused on a name he recognised and worked his way around that section of the map.

The name that had come into his view was not his own but his mother's, Lilian, which was all present and correct. But as he worked his eyes away from her entry, he started to realise what the problem was. He then focused on his father's details. Something was wrong. Colin didn't fully realise what was actually wrong and he reverted back to his mother's condition – was she upset because she had seen his father's name, or because there was something incorrect with the details? Colin studied the information further. He wondered whether the name was wrong but that was as he knew it to be.

However, as he delved deeper into the information, a slight variation became clear. According to the tree, his father had died the year before Colin's own arrival into the world. He read the entry again…and again. The fact that the tree indicated that Colin's father possibly wasn't his actual father was probably why his mother was so upset. His immediate reaction was to assume that the dates were wrong and that his father had died the following year. Colin thought he knew that his own birthday was correct, so it had to be a typo error and that had just opened his mother's floodgates, as she had been reminded of her husband's demise.

By now his mother had stopped her erratic sobbing and had composed herself and turned to look up at her son. There was an apologetic look in her eyes that was likely to bring unpleasant news.

"I'm sorry," she said, "...but before you ask, I'm afraid it's true; the dates are correct. Your father died before you were born. The fourteen-month gap is correct. Your father is not your father."

Colin took this statement as an opportunity to slowly sit down next to his mother. For a moment he had hoped that his father was still his father, and that some other scenario would explain the situation and make them both feel better. But her words were indicative of something more final; something he didn't want to hear. He chose to sit as he felt he might otherwise fall.

His mind began to race in several different directions at once: *Why had he previously been told something that had obviously been false? ...Why had this information not been corrected before now, and how had he been alive for nearly 50 years as part of a lie?... Why had his cousin been stupid enough to do a family tree and think it wise to circulate it to everybody in the world?!*

It hadn't been sent to everybody in the world but that is what it felt like to Colin, who by now had gone both cold and hot with a mixture of fear, rage and puzzlement.

Colin felt compelled to ask the obvious question: "Who is

my father, then?"

His mother looked up at him with sorrowful eyes. They were distorted by a thin layer of water that had started to collect in the recesses of her lower eyelids.

"Is it really important to know all the details? Wouldn't you be happier just remembering what you think you know?"

"No, I don't!" exclaimed Colin, with both rage and with an urgency to get up from his sitting position to confront his mother. She had started the lie and she was going to explain everything!

His mother nervously followed Colin's command and reluctantly started the process.

"First of all, your father did die as you were told, but we had split up. He went back to sea and I moved out of the Naval Quarters and got a job as an auxiliary in a nearby hospital, and moved nearby."

After fifty years it was difficult for her to refer to her husband as anything other than Colin's father, and despite the obvious historical error, Colin let her continue.

"Whilst I was there, I… I was attacked by an acquaintance and …and you were the result. I'm sorry I cannot say this in any other way. I just need to get it out!"

Colin could feel the fifty years of frustration and hurt in her voice, and for a minute he felt some sympathy, but he was the one that had been lied to. He had been quite happy for most of his life, knowing that his father was dead and proud that his mother had managed to bring him up as a normal human being. But now he knew he wasn't so normal. He was hurt, he was angry. He didn't feel right anymore.

Colin sat back down next to his mother.

"So, who is my biological father…and is he still alive?" was the resultant reply from Colin, who chose to ignore his mother's earlier rebuff.

His mother didn't really want to continue the conversation but felt obliged to give some form of response:

"I don't know if he's still alive, and he was just somebody I knew only briefly. I have tried to block it from my memory."

Colin knew that in his line of work memories could be blocked by the mind to protect it, but he also knew that the family tree had unlocked the door, and even if his mother didn't want to remember, or couldn't remember, she soon would. He didn't press the matter and decided to await her guilt rising to the surface of her memory.

"I'm going upstairs to change," he said, and slowly rose from the settee and exited the room, leaving his mother to dwell on her true history. As he ascended the stairs, he heard her start to sob again.

As a loving son he should have turned around and retraced his steps back into the room where his mother was sitting, but he didn't. He needed to gather his thoughts away from the sobbing, and so made his way to his bedroom at the top of the stairs and flopped onto his bed, flinging his whole body back so that he was looking up at the ceiling.

The ceiling was meant to give him something to focus on. The swirl of the plaster pattern hid a myriad of mystic meanings. He couldn't remember the last time that he had laid back on his bed during the day for solace, but he had found that by doing so it helped to clear his mind and concentrate on his problems. He now had a big one that was racing around inside of him. He wasn't who he thought he was; he was only fifty percent Colin

Smith, and even that assumed that his mother wasn't lying any further, and that she was his actual birth mother. At this point he couldn't really fathom what he was meant to think. If you are not who you think you are, how are you supposed to react? Colin took a deep breath and tried to focus on something positive: *What if his biological father was a Noble Prize Winner or a famous athlete? Would that soften the blow?*

Little can counteract a five decade lie and consequently Colin reverted to 'anger mode', which was surprising for somebody who had been trained to be patient and understanding in his line of work.

His thought process was interrupted by the appearance of his mother at the bedroom doorway. She was holding a mug of tea in each hand. It was obvious that this was a peace offering and an opportunity to talk further. The hysterical reactions would have passed and it was now time for some comforting debate. In all the commotion Colin didn't realise that there was another person in the equation of hurt; his mother had likely been raped and that should be of far more concern than his own fifty per cent dilution.

He beckoned her to approach the bed and he dutifully reached out a hand to receive the offering, whilst using his other elbow to raise his body to an upright position. He swung his legs around away from the bed to facilitate some space for his mother to sit down. She took up the offer and placed her mug on the adjacent bedside table. They smiled at each other, and despite Colin holding a mug of hot tea, the couple embraced in a carefully orchestrated manner. The tea remained in the mug as the two parted following their reconciliation.

His mother broke the silence:

"Do you really need to know who your biological father is?" she said with sorrowful eyes. They had the characteristic redness around them that was evident of an outpouring of grief. Colin took a sip of tea from his mug, which somehow made the situation more tolerable.

"I'm not sure," he replied, "one part of me needs to get over the shock and think rationally, the other wants to know so that I can find out who I am."

"You are who you are and that is made up of more than just who your biological parents are. You have developed as a person despite not having a father by your side. We have just given you the start; you have made yourself who you are and it shouldn't matter what happened fifty or so years ago."

There was a degree of logic to what Colin's mother had said and for the time being Colin agreed with her synopsis. His mother had obviously tried to forget the incident as the decades passed and she had probably succeeded; he would have to try to do the same. But of continuing concern was his mother's suggestion that he was the result of something sinister, something which may have been against his mother's will. Not only was he illegitimate, he was probably the result of an unreported crime.

Further confusing thoughts fired through his brain at such an alarming rate that he hadn't finished asking himself a question before another had started. There was a jumble of words in his head that needed to be re-arranged and eventually concluded. He wanted to know, yet he didn't want to upset his mother any further by continuing with his interrogation. He would probably have to have the information drip-fed to him over a period of time. Or he could just accept his new found position and move on with his life.

CHAPTER FIVE
Progress

Friday arrived and Colin found himself parking outside his appointment. He was visiting Sam and Josie again. Despite his confrontation with his own mother, the intervening days had mellowed almost as if there was an unwritten truce, but maybe it was the calm before a storm. The family tree had been put away in a cupboard so that it couldn't reignite the situation, but nonetheless both parties knew it was a potential fire hazard in their lives.

Colin opened his car door and exited towards the front of the house. He pressed the button on his key fob and there was the pleasing 'beep'. He had to park slightly further away than his last visit, and as he approached the front door he managed to catch a glimpse of Sam looking out of his bedroom window. His expression was slightly different; there was a vague look of surprise and Colin wondered whether Sam hadn't seen him pull up but had heard the 'beep', which had startled him.

Josie had obviously been aware of Colin's impending arrival and the front door was already being opened as he approached.

"Good Morning," they said in unison, which put a matching grin on both of their faces. Colin was ushered into the front room for an update on the activities since his last visit.

"How's he been?" he enquired.

"Pretty much the same," answered Josie, as she beckoned Colin to sit on the sofa, "but he did seem a bit more alive. I'm not sure if you did something or whether he anticipated your visit but this morning his face looked less gaunt. There was still no meaningful expression but he just appeared less dead in his appearance."

Josie didn't like to use those terms but Colin was pleased that her vocabulary was beginning to show signs that death was an inevitable outcome for her scenario. She may not have realised that she was becoming more accepting but Colin knew that progress was being made on her side of the equation.

"Okay, let me pop up and see him!" he said in an almost excited manner, and with those words still echoing around the room, he got up from the sofa and climbed the stairs towards Sam's bedroom.

This time he didn't wait for Josie to lead his path but she chose to stay downstairs and shouted upwards that Colin was on his way. There was no response from upstairs; Colin didn't expect one but he did the correct thing and knocked on Sam's door before pushing it ajar and entering the room.

Sam looked at him. It was his normal look, but it was at the same time slightly different. Josie was right, there had been a change. Colin wanted to label it an improvement. He duly sat down on the stool next to Sam's bed. Sam hadn't changed his position, and so Colin found himself looking at the side of Sam's head as he continued to look towards the doorway that Colin had just entered.

"How are you?" asked Colin, in order to start some form of process. "Where is your blue car?" was the response.

Colin realised that his original thoughts were correct; he had parked out of Sam's view. "Is it important to you?" asked Colin, trying to maintain the conversation.

"I like it. Did you buy it from Uncle Jack?" enquired Sam.

Colin thought before answering and suggested that he move the car into view. Sam turned his head and agreed.

"Okay, stay there and I'll move it for you."

Colin got up from the chair and didn't run downstairs but didn't amble either. He needed to maintain the momentum of the earlier discussion and so, as he reached the bottom of the stairs quicker than normal, he smiled at Josie who had positioned herself in his path with a look of panic on her face.

"What's wrong?" she exclaimed.

"Nothing," replied Colin, "I just need to move the car into view."

And with that announcement he opened the front door to complete the task. Luckily, he could park across the drive and still be seen from the bedroom window, so he edged the car as far forward as he could, without nudging the car that was parked directly outside the house, and where he had parked previously. With the task completed, he returned to the house via the path and proceeded back to the upstairs area where he hoped Sam would be awaiting him. As he entered the bedroom, he could see that the car was nicely positioned in view.

"There you go," he said, in anticipation of some form of approval or, if not approval, then some form of acknowledgement. The acknowledgement arrived but it wasn't in the form of a traditional 'thank you'; merely the start of a vocal questioning:

"Is it Uncle Jack's? Have you seen him and did he let you

borrow the car, or have you bought it from him? You must have cleaned it as the shade of blue is different…"

Colin was thinking as Sam was questioning him. Having said previously to Josie that she should not try to fight nor correct Sam but just roll with what he said, Colin found himself making a choice about where he could take the conversation; purchase or borrow?

"I bought it from him," he replied, on the basis that if he had borrowed it, there would have to be a point in time when he would have to return it. At the moment the car was the key to unlocking a response from Sam; if the key was lost, then so could Colin's task of easing Sam's pain. In any case, Colin would have to drive something to the house and he wasn't planning on changing his car yet. Buying the car seemed the right thing to say. It was a lie, obviously, but a necessary one.

"When did you buy it?"

Colin paused for a bit. He didn't want to be in a position of offering potential hope of Sam meeting Uncle Jack again by answering that the purchase was recent.

"Oh, I've had the car a couple of years now," was the best he could come up with in the short space of time allowed.

"Oh," replied Sam in a vaguely disappointed voice, which was only just discernible from his normal speech.

The conversation seemed to stop there, as there was no continuation in Sam's response and the room fell into a strange silence.

"What did you like about the car?" enquired Colin, hoping that he could kick-start the conversation again, but it looked as though depression had kicked Sam into touch as there was no response.

Colin tried several more questions: "Do you think it looks better clean?... When was the last time you went in the car?... How long is it since you saw Uncle Jack?" But each request was met with a gaunt stare that seemed to be the default position for Sam. The vague flicker of facial hope had left him on the news that Uncle Jack's car was no longer in his possession, and Colin supposed that with that piece of news Sam registered that Uncle Jack was unlikely to be seen again.

Colin therefore raised himself from the chair and exited the room, saying his goodbye to Sam. As previously, there was no corresponding response.

Josie had obviously heard movement and was anxiously waiting at the foot of the stairs. Colin indicated that he would like to go into the front room to speak about the situation, and he followed her to the sofa, where they positioned themselves at different ends but facing each other.

"He seems keen on this Uncle Jack character. Is he still alive?"

"No," replied Josie, "he died several years ago. He was my grandfather's brother – he lived locally and used to stay here in-between jobs, marriages, drunken brawls…he wasn't a particularly stable person, but dad obviously latched onto him."

"So, is your grandfather still with us; Sam's father?"

"Yes, he is… but he emigrated to Florida several years ago, married his second wife, and doesn't come back to England. He'd be ninety-something now and I doubt if he could travel even if he wanted to. He knows that Sam is unwell and does phone occasionally but we haven't seen him in about fifteen or sixteen years. We were all going to go out to Florida and see him but it never happened for obvious reasons," responded

Josie, jerking her head slightly in an upward motion to verify that Sam had prevented the plan from taking place.

Colin remained pensive for a moment and then remarked:

"Does your grandfather ever speak to Sam over the phone?"

"The last time was several years ago. Neither recognised each other's voices and I think it would be too upsetting for Sam's father to hear how far he has actually declined since. We of course have told him but it's worse if you experience it first-hand, so we haven't pushed it. I'm not sure how much longer either has, and I suppose rather selfishly I'd like to think that their own memories of each other should be left where they are. Any last memory would be strong enough to wipe out all the others."

Josie was right; if you see a loved one suffering during their last days, that is the image that overtakes all others, so it would probably be best not to chance any encounter. Colin had thought that perhaps the grandfather could pretend to be Uncle Jack, but that would really be for Colin's benefit of the overall case study, and he was pretty sure that Sam would be expecting to hear a younger voice, rather than a ninety-year-old one. It was a stupid idea that was quickly removed from the thought process.

Colin plucked up the courage to ask a huge favour:

"Could I ask you to enquire whether your grandfather would be willing to speak to me about his brother? I know it's probably not what you are expecting but if I could get some more first-hand knowledge of Uncle Jack, then I may be able to bring Sam out of his shell a bit more. At the moment, Uncle Jack and his blue Ford are the only things that seem to ignite him. Oh, I've also told Sam that I bought my car from Uncle

Jack a couple of years ago."

Josie looked in surprise at Colin before he continued:

"Yes, it seemed appropriate to give Sam something to latch onto, and me purchasing Uncle Jack's car seemed temporarily to spark him into life…but I've reached a block at the moment."

"I'm not sure if my grandfather would be up for talking about Sam," replied Josie with a degree of hesitation in her voice, which implied that she really didn't want to proceed with Colin's plan, but she didn't know how to refuse him either.

Colin realised that this situation was a strain and so he quickly interjected:

"How about I approach the conversation on the basis that I am writing a book on some of the characters from the past, and that Jack has been brought to my attention as being a lively soul in the community and worthy of mention. The chances are that your grandfather will spark into life; they can always remember more from the past than they can from yesterday, and I could get some useful pointers to helping your father."

This seemed to do the trick, as Josie reluctantly looked up and nodded in agreement to the latest suggestion.

Colin continued with the process:

"Would you like to phone him and pass the phone over to me, or would you prefer if I phone him from my office; they're five hours behind us, aren't they?"

Josie looked pensive for a moment, as if she was trying to find a way out of what she had just agreed to.

"I'll phone," she said, "if only to get his acceptance to you contacting him direct at a time that would suit you both."

Colin looked pleased with the outcome; Josie didn't.

Colin wasn't sure if this was due to that side of the family not really being very helpful in the past, or whether there was some other reason, but the day was concluded there and Josie agreed to contact Colin with the relevant phone number when she had cleared it with her grandfather.

The normal goodbyes were exchanged and Colin made his way out of the house, up the path to the top of the driveway. As he approached his car, he purposely dropped his keys that were in his left hand. They fell behind him, giving him the opportunity to turn around and glance up at Sam's window. Unfortunately, he glanced up when he was at the lowest point of his swoop, and consequently if he continued to glance in Sam's direction, it would no longer be a glance but an obvious stare, so Colin aborted that part of his plan. He'd have to practice that move again.

He instead proceeded up the path and got into his car and pretended to adjust the rear-view mirror, which luckily was directly in the line of sight between himself and Sam's bedroom. He could see the top part of Sam's head facing in his general direction, which gave him hope that if he could speak to someone who could provide some stories about Uncle Jack, then that could help to progress the situation. Colin started the car and proceeded to drive off down the road towards his next appointment.

CHAPTER SIX
Long Distance, Long Memory

The following morning Colin received a phone call from Josie at just after nine. She seemed in a better mood and was almost cheerful. Colin decided not to remark on her demeanour for fear of alienating her, or somehow insulting her by comparing her attitude with the previous day.

"Morning Josie," he said in response to her initial words.

"I've got that phone number for you. If I text it to you, you'll have it correctly stored, and I'll add the access code so that it will work okay," volunteered Josie.

Colin was pleasantly surprised that she had agreed to give him the number but also that she had presumably contacted her grandfather so quickly.

"…his name is George. Try and phone after two, our time. I've positioned it that you are writing a book about local characters from his era and that you may want to hear about a young Jack. He says he has some stories that he can now tell as Jack is no longer with us! I have no idea what they could be, and I'm not sure that I want to know either, but I'll leave it up to you how you play it. Anyway, he's expecting your call over the next couple of days. I've got to go as there's somebody at the front door. Bye."

Colin heard the accompanying silence in his ear and thought to himself that his day was perhaps off to a good start. He was due to be out on appointments for most of the day but he was sure that he had a gap at about 2.30pm that would provide an opportunity for him to make the call. He therefore started to think about what he wanted to say, or rather what he thought he needed to know, to get Sam to open up a bit more.

Whilst both he and Josie knew that Sam would never get better, it was incumbent upon him to ensure that Sam's demise was made as comfortable as possible. Any engagement that resulted from his work would hopefully help the family through this troublesome time. In-between appointments Colin could scribble down some notes around what he needed to know and how he would get them into the conversation, which he wanted to be just that; a conversation rather than an interrogation.

By comparison to Sam's case, his other case studies were in some ways no different; a terminally declining person was always the subject, and in most cases, there was the same theme of a backward step into early memories, which had sacrificed most of the recent events to compensate. It was in Colin's opinion a sort of time travel, where early memories became the 'now' and 'now' became easily forgotten. His main job was to add some sense to the whole procedure and minimise on the suffering of both the patient and their families, who often witnessed a person they knew transform into somebody who was both physically unrecognisable and who was living in an age before the family was even born. Frustration was always the key aspect for the families; bewilderment for the patient. Somehow Colin had to meet the two in the middle so that life could be a little more normal.

However, with Sam he had never known a case study where there was such a fixation on one particular scenario; Uncle Jack and his blue Ford. With his other cases repetition was common but there would be several topics that would flash in and out of numerous short-lived conversations. There would be meals, school friends, football matches, wallpaper, fishing trips, holidays, first loves and a whole host of other memories. With Sam it was as if Uncle Jack and his blue Ford were the only things that had happened to him during whatever period he was currently living in. Or the memories were so strong and important that all other thoughts from the same era were being squeezed out to make room. It was a strange case indeed and it deserved the extra effort to conclude it.

When the afternoon arrived, Colin found himself sitting in his car around the corner from his 3.00pm appointment. He was 45 minutes early and this provided the opportunity to make the call. He had scribbled down a variety of topics onto an A4 notepad, his phone was resting in its hands-free cradle, and the relevant international phone number was already displayed on the screen. Colin pressed the green handset symbol and awaited the call connecting.

Unfortunately, instead of being greeted by a ring tone and ultimately a person at the other end, Colin was confronted with a three-note, high-pitched tone, followed by a woman's voice declaring to him in a schoolteacher manner, that his call could not be connected as international calls were not permitted from his phone.

"Bugger!" he said out loud to himself, which clearly shook the small terrier that had just started to relieve itself against the adjacent tree to where Colin had parked, as the dog stopped in mid flow, and both it and its owner scuttled off to the next available upright. Colin both grinned and frowned at the same time.

He quickly cancelled the call and fumbled through the various settings in his phone, trying desperately to find the section which would enable him to override his current parameters.

"Bugger!" he said again, as his panic contrived to lead him to everywhere but where he needed to actually be. Luckily this time there was no animal for him to upset.

In desperation Colin hit a pre-determined number which directed him to a supposedly helpful assistant at his office. After several rings the phone was eventually answered by Julie, a thirty-something year old colleague, who thought she knew it all, but who had only been in the department for four months. Colin didn't bother exchanging pleasantries and jumped straight in with his request, which probably sounded more like a demand at the other end of the phone.

"Julie, can you tell me how I make a call to Florida from my company phone?" There was definitely an air of desperation which was picked up by Julie. "Slow down boy, why do you need to know that?!"

"I just need to contact a relation in the Sam case and they're in Florida, and my bloody phone says that such calls are not permitted from this phone. How do I rectify that?"

Colin's reply was a bit more controlled but still there was an air of frustrated importance about it. "Well, you'll need the Director's approval and then the phone company needs to be contacted to override the current restriction. He's out at the moment and not due back until the end of the day."

This wasn't what Colin wanted to hear and his frustration culminated in a familiar fashion: "Bugger!"

"I didn't hear that," remarked Julie, who obviously had.

"Don't worry, I'll get clearance tomorrow and make the call then instead," and without waiting for a response, Colin hit the 'end call' icon and the line went back to silent.

In typical movie fashion, Colin sunk his head into the steering wheel in front of him. Luckily the horn button wasn't in the middle but on the end of the right-hand indicator stalk. His head rested there for a second or two and then he slowly raised it up, as if his torso was being unrolled. There was a slight twinkle in his eye as he realised that he had his personal phone with him. He had used that before to call a friend who was on holiday in Spain. Bingo!

He fumbled in his briefcase and at the bottom was his trusted phone. He switched it on and awaited the screen coming to life. His only potential problem was the life left in the battery but the screen clearly showed sufficient juice to make the call. He looked at his watch to check the time. Ten minutes had somehow disappeared since he had parked the car.

To make sure that he had the correct number to call, he forwarded the text that Josie had sent to him and there was the satisfying 'ping' as his own phone received the required information. He hurriedly fumbled through his phone's menu options and retrieved the new message. The Florida number was underlined, inviting him to press the area accordingly. Colin pressed and held the phone to his ear.

There was a delay, but eventually a ring tone was heard. It wasn't one he had heard before but he assumed that he was on track okay.

"Hello," broke the procedure.

"Hello," replied Colin, "could I speak to George, please?"

"That's me," came the reply, which was most reassuring to Colin, as not only had he managed to get through first time, but also there was an underlying air of comfort in the voice at the other end; a mixture of English and American fused accents.

"Excellent! Hi, I'm Colin Smith, I believe Josie informed you that I would try and call you to talk about your brother Jack and the area you were both living in? Is now a good time to talk?"

In his excitement he had forgotten about the pleasantries of 'How are you' and the normal British opener about the weather. Nevertheless, there didn't seem to be any hostility from the other end of the phone.

"Yes, yes, Josie did say something. How is she?"

"Well, she seems to be coping a bit better," replied Colin, but perhaps he had answered the wrong question, as George was asking about her general demeanour rather than specifically about her life with Sam.

"Good," was the hesitant reply, as if Colin had indeed got the wrong approach. Colin went for broke:

"I'd like you to think back to when Jack was younger and when he was living in the area. I think he was quite close to your son, Samuel…"

"I'm not sure that I should! Jack was a bit of a naughty lad; got into a lot of trouble and unfortunately he sometimes took Sam with him on his adventures. I'm not proud and we had trouble with Sam as a result. There are things that perhaps shouldn't be said, but as it's so long ago I suppose there's no harm in talking about some of them now. I'd just ask you to be a bit tactful in what you let Josie know, as she probably wouldn't want to hear some of the bad stuff about her father."

Colin thought he should politely interject at this point:

"Are you sure that you are okay with this? You'll appreciate that I am trying to write a book about the local area and some of the characters that lived in it, but if you think that your stories will be too upsetting for Josie then don't tell me."

It was fairly evident that this was probably more about George getting things off of his chest and releasing some guilty secrets and finding peace himself, rather than directly helping Colin with his phantom book. Sometimes talking to a stranger – particularly one that is four thousand miles away – can be a better cleanser than keeping secrets stashed away inside one's self.

Colin prepared himself for the onslaught and hurriedly tried to find the car charger for his phone, as he was now anticipating a long session. Luckily the cable attachment was with him, and he plugged the socket end into the cigarette lighter hole and connected the small pin at the other end into the base of his phone, all whilst resting the handset between his shoulder and the side of his head. He turned the ignition on for good measure. There was a satisfying 'ping' that indicated power was flowing. George responded:

"No, I'm good. This needs to be said, so it might as well be you that hears it…"

"Okay, I'm good if you're good," replied Colin, taking up the American expression by accident. He waited.

"My brother was a rebel. The family had a lot of trouble with him; breaking into property, theft, assault. He had a very unstable life, which I and the rest of the family distanced ourselves from. When he eventually went to prison for a 6-month spell, we gathered our thoughts and devised a plan to help him try and get back onto the straight and narrow. However, when he came out, he seemed to be a changed man. The underlying aggression had disappeared and he managed to hold down a job in a local factory. The money wasn't good but it gave him a focus and a purpose. He seemed to stop drifting into trouble and shortly afterwards he and Sam got friendly. Sam must have been in his early teens or so, and Jack would take him fishing and watched him play cricket, go to the cinema and that sort of thing. That's when he bought the blue Ford Cortina that Josie said Sam had recalled. Maybe Sam is associating those good times with the car…"

Colin felt obliged to say something, if only to confirm that he was still listening, but in letting down his guard too easily he didn't realise that he was about to negate his phantom writing requirement and reverse the conversation into his interest in Sam:

"Yes, the blue car seems to be what Sam has latched onto. I've had to tell him that I bought it from Jack to maintain our line of communication. Do you know how long he had the car for, and was there a subsequent car that came into the equation?"

"Oh, you've spoken to my son, why would you do that? Colin had to think quickly:

"I met Josie and your son at a local event when Sam noticed my blue car, so I thought it best to go along with his wishes and I made up a story to fit his thoughts."

Colin grimaced as he rolled out another lie.

"Oh, okay," was the rather accepting response.

Colin quickly interjected to put the conversation back onto his intended path: "You were saying…"

"Oh yes, he had the car for some time until…well until…until he had to get rid of it, and he bought a red Vauxhall of some description. I can't remember what it was exactly but it was a smaller thing. After that Sam got his own car and became more independent and the two drifted apart, thank God, although they did see each other on the odd occasion but it was far less regular."

Colin was a bit surprised by the last statement and felt he had to enquire further: "You seem happy that the two parted company, did they have an argument?"

"No. Well maybe. I'm not sure I should tell you…Josie doesn't need to know this, so keep this bit to yourself."

Colin nodded, as if this could somehow be seen over the phone. "Of course," he replied.

"Okay. I'm not proud to say this but Jack came back into our lives a couple of years later and sometimes stayed overnight. At one point we took in lodgers to get some money into the house and Sam used to help out. Jack and Sam had been out for a drink and came home a bit worse for wear. I was out with the wife; we were at some event somewhere and we came back after Sam and Jack had got in. Anyway, the following day the lodger said to my wife that she had been attacked. My wife naturally assumed that Jack had flipped back into his old ways and so kicked him out of the house and he never returned. I'm afraid that there's more to the story but I really can't say anything else."

Colin felt obliged to jump in and rescue George from his obvious pain. Sam had already regressed past this point so it wasn't relevant to his quest of travelling back in time with him. Colin needed to know what his life was like before these harrowing events.

"George, thank you for that painful story. That can't have been easy for you. What about when Jack was younger?"

"Well, he was like any other tearaway; only worse. Hated school but loved sports like cricket and football. But my parents had a lot of trouble with him… and to be honest he was always a wrong 'un."

It was obvious to Colin that he wasn't going to get any more useful information from the conversation, as he was learning more unsavoury things about Uncle Jack and nothing about Sam. He would have to make do with what he had already gleaned and so thought about how he could end the conversation without appearing too unfriendly. He had basically learnt nothing further about Sam or Jack, except that Jack's next car was probably a red one and that he was definitely somebody that Sam shouldn't have got involved with. But Jack was the only potential conduit that Colin could use, so he would have to persevere down that route.

"George, thanks for that. If you don't mind, I'll write up some notes, and if I may, I'll ask Josie to contact you if I need to speak to you again. Is that okay?"

On reflection, Colin thought that he had been too abrupt, but his three 'o' clock appointment was beckoning and he realised that this current well was now dry. To his surprise there was nothing but acceptance from George, who replied positively:

"Yes, of course. Nice speaking to you."

The call then ended and Colin sank back into his seat, realising that he had just wasted several minutes of his life, and probably several pounds of long-distance phone credit. He gathered his thoughts and briefly glanced at the notes for his impending meeting. It was 3.05, so he quickly transformed himself into a professional manner and exited his car and strolled around the corner to his next appointment, pressing the button on his key fob; 'beep!'

CHAPTER SEVEN
Blue Car Blues

It was the following week and Colin arrived at Josie's front door. It was raining and he had to rush from his car to her house. He was expected, but unusually Josie was not at an already open door and Colin had to press the illuminated bell push on the door frame. He could hear the corresponding chimes coming from inside the house but couldn't recognise the tune. He could also hear the hurried footsteps of the occupant, who had presumably been reminded of his visit.

A flustered Josie answered the door in an apologetic manner. "Sorry, bit of trouble with dad but he's okay now."

Josie ushered Colin into the downstairs lounge and moved her right arm to indicate that he should sit in the single chair. She took up a position on the sofa.

"What's the trouble?" asked Colin.

"Dad was panicking that you weren't coming but he quietened down when you pulled up outside. He must really like your car."

Colin was slightly surprised but thought it wise to continue the conversation around the subject.

"Yes, he does seem to like the car. I spoke to your grandfather and got a few bits of information but I'm afraid nothing much of use. It looks like Uncle Jack was a bit of a rogue; the proverbial black sheep."

"Yes, I've heard stories," interjected Josie.

Colin thought that he shouldn't elaborate so took the conversation down a more professional route. "The car and Uncle Jack seem to be the only key, so I'll pop upstairs and see if I can get any further benefit from continuing down that road."

Colin got up from his seat and Josie let him travel up the stairs unaccompanied but shouted from a distance that he was on his way.

Colin knocked on the door before entering Sam's room and viewed the vista. His car was again parked in a suitable position but the rain rather obscured the view. But as Sam had recognised it and its arrival, Colin assumed that he could start the conversation:

"Hello Sam, I thought I'd come and see you again."

Sam didn't say anything and continued to stare out of the window. He had the same gaunt expression that would probably never leave him. They sat in silence and Colin wondered whether he had done something wrong. As Josie told him that Sam had been awaiting his arrival, Colin thought he'd stretch the truth:

"Sorry I'm late, the rain slows everything down."

"I don't like the rain…" replied Sam unexpectedly, "…it means we have to come in from the field and put the covers on the wicket. We then have to wait and just sit drinking juice. I don't mind juice…I just prefer playing cricket."

"When was the last time you played?" asked Colin, wishing to continue the flow.

"It was yesterday. Luckily, we won so we didn't need to play today. I would like to play today but it's raining so I'll stay in. I always stay in when it's raining."

"When are you playing again?" enquired Colin.

"I don't know. If it's raining, then we won't play but if it isn't, then we will."

"Where do you play?"

"At the school field but I'm now in bed so I won't play."

Colin struggled to keep the conversation on track, as it was evident that Sam hadn't played cricket yesterday, or probably any day in the last couple of decades, but he had to keep up the illusion that was being recalled in Sam's mind.

"Who else is normally in the cricket team with you?"

"Nobody if it's raining…we don't play when it's raining."

"But what if it isn't raining, who is in the team with you?"

"We don't play when it's raining, so nobody is in the team. We just drink juice."

It was becoming a repetitive loop, and whilst any frustrated parent would shout out the many inaccuracies in Sam's words, Colin's training meant that he kept a calm demeanour and developed another angle of questioning:

"Does Uncle Jack take you to the cricket match?"
"Sometimes."

"What, in the blue car?"

"Yes, sometimes."

"Do you like going in the blue car?"

"Yes, if it's the blue car. But I don't like the red one. It's not shiny. It's not a Ford. I like Ford cars. I like blue Ford cars that are shiny."

Colin realised that the red car was probably the one that Josie's grandfather had mentioned in his telephone conversation.

If so, he could probably pinpoint the era if he could get Josie to ask her grandfather for a few more details. He continued:

"I have a blue car…"

"Yes, I like blue cars."

But that was the end of the conversation, as abruptly it came to a halt and Colin's metaphorical coin had run out. The machine he had been playing reverted to sleep mode awaiting the next time. So, after making some notes and realising that the machine had probably been unplugged too, he gathered his thoughts, said his goodbye and exited Sam's room and wandered downstairs to a waiting Josie, who was at the foot of the stairs having been alerted by Colin's footsteps.

"Anything?" she said with a slight plea in her voice.

Colin ushered her into the front room and pushed the door towards its frame so as they could be more private. Apart from Sam, there was nobody else in the house, but he thought it wise to take that precaution.

"Can you do me a favour?" he asked.

"Sure, what?" was the response.

"Could you phone your grandfather again? I don't want to do it as I nearly blew my story last time, but your grandfather mentioned that his brother changed his blue Ford for a smaller red car at some point. Could you find out when that was? I'd like it fairly accurate if you can."

"Sure, but why?" was the natural response.

"It seems as though your dad is remembering a red car that Uncle Jack had when he got rid of his blue Ford, which your dad liked so much. He shouldn't be remembering that sort of event unless it was really important. Either his memory is more flexible than I thought it should be; that is, he is living in a period of time that may flip in and out over a several year period, or he's getting older in his head rather than travelling further back in time, which would be the more normal procedure in these sorts of cases. I'm thinking that your dad is about twelve in his head but the red car may be a memory from when he was in his teens. Could you have a go at finding out?"

Josie nodded approvingly and the faintest expression of joy darted across her face. Colin hoped that the expression wasn't one of false hope that her father was getting better. Maybe she was just glad to do some detective work rather than housework.

The pair duly parted and Colin would set off for home but - as normal - he always tried to glimpse casually up at the bedroom window to see if Sam was in view. He was.

Colin's drive home was normally a drab affair. The rain had continued to drop from the sky in volumes that were hard to comprehend. It wasn't particularly heavy rain but it was persistent. It rained for hours and hours with such a continuation that it was inevitable that the drains would become clogged and the roads would be covered with a thin film of water, which made driving difficult, if not dangerous in places. It was therefore no surprise that Colin's accident-free driving record of nearly thirty years would come to an abrupt end, as whilst he had been paying particular attention to the driving conditions, the driver of a large white van exiting from a side road on his left, had obviously been elsewhere in his own head.

The van slid into the left-hand side of Colin's car, pushing it into the slow-moving oncoming traffic on the other side of the road. There were multiple bangs and thuds mixed with the sound of breaking glass that seemed to go on forever, as the traffic on both sides of the road found it impossible to avoid their neighbours. There were screams from the nearby pedestrians and groans and curses from the vehicle's occupants. Colin was alive but shaken, and probably banged his head on the driver's side window. He looked around the interior of his car. Anything that wasn't screwed or glued was now in a different place. Notebooks and pens were now in foot-wells and jackets and sandwich boxes were now sitting in novel positions. Carefully collected sweet wrappers, which over time had been confined to ashtrays, were now merrily exploring other areas of the car.

The engine of Colin's car had stopped and the only sound he could now hear was his own heartbeat that lay amplified in his chest. Gradually drivers and passengers exited from their cars to survey the situation and Colin thought he should do the same. He tried to remember what handle or button to use to formulate his escape. Without looking he reached out with his right hand and flicked the necessary handle. Fortunately, the door opened as it should but it could only swing out so far as its progress was halted by the front of a dark green vehicle. There was just enough room for Colin to extract himself and he stood up in the middle of the road to look at the carnage. So fuddled was he, that he forgot about the rain which was still falling from the sky, and it was some while before he twisted round to retrieve his raincoat from the rear of the car. Luckily the rear door also opened as intended, but in hurriedly swinging the coat around him he let a flurry of sweet paper confetti fly into the air.

Looking around him, he could now see that about eight vehicles had been involved in the accident. The white van that had caused all the carnage, was embedded in the left-hand side of Colin's car and his car had in turn ended up touching the dark green car on the opposite side of the road. Colin and the driver of the dark green car exchanged glances, which conveyed that both were okay, and Colin then turned his attention to the idiot that had hit him. Now that the shock had dissipated his body, he thought it right to convey his thoughts to the driver of the white van. He hadn't prepared anything in his head; he was just going to blow his top and probably swear a lot. However, that joy would have to be for another day, as it was evident that the driver of the white van had decided that he wasn't going to be present for any enquiry or exchange of opinions. He had left by foot in a hurry and Colin surmised that he had been hit by a stolen vehicle and a likely uninsured driver. His frustration at not being able to vent his anger was curtailed by the arriving sirens and blue flashing lights that indicated that the cavalry had arrived.

    The first voices to speak to him were the ambulance crew. They had parked a couple of vehicle lengths behind him. They were a young couple, probably in their mid-twenties; a man and a woman, who both had concerned expressions on their faces. Colin assumed that their concerned faces were part of the uniform, but those expressions continued as he was ferried to the back of the ambulance and made to sit down on the long bench on the right-hand side of the interior. A large white gauze had been hurriedly placed on the right-hand side of his head, and as the ambulance crew removed it, Colin looked down to see that a large patch of red had presumably exited from his head. Colin gulped in cartoon style and slowly fell back onto the remaining area of the bench, unaware that his injuries were not as bad as they looked. He consequently wasn't aware of the ensuing exchange between the ambulance crew.

"I think it's just his ear that has torn in the impact. It's external rather than internal but we should ferry this one back to base for a look over."

The recipient agreed by nodding and indicated that they would see to any of the other potential hospital bound victims, whilst their colleague remained in the ambulance with Colin, who by now had started to re-enter the current world.

"Ooh! How long have I been gone?" said Colin from a semi-horizontal position.

"Literally a minute. Probably the shock of the blood but don't worry, you've just ruptured the outer rim of your ear, but we'll get you back to the hospital just to make sure that it's nothing more serious."

Those were comforting words, which were accompanied by the application of a temporary glue-like substance to the offending area of Colin's right ear. That sealed the area from further bleeding.

By now there were several ambulances at the scene, together with numerous police cars and a fire engine for good measure. The myriad of flashing blue lights rebounded off of every reflective surface, so much so that Colin had to look away from the rear opening of the ambulance and directed his gaze to the front of the rear cabin where the light show was dulled by the matt interior finish. But curiosity forced him to reverse his stance as his companion assisted another walking wounded into the back of the vehicle. Colin smiled and nodded in the direction of his fellow victim. She was thirty years old, or thereabouts, and Colin partially recognised her. At first, he didn't realise from where but it became apparent that she had been driving the dark green car that Colin had been pushed into. He felt compelled to offer his apologies:

"Sorry," he said, in a rather sheepish way.

"Oh gosh, it's not your fault, it was that bloody idiot in the van!"

The reply was filled with a mixture of venom and frustration which didn't match with the calm appearance of her exterior. She too was shaken.

"Ear," said Colin, pointing with his right hand to his sealed appendage.

"Elbow," came the reply, this time in a more controlled manner, "I think it's just badly bruised."

She held up her right arm to afford Colin a better view, and he could see that the swelling around her elbow area was probably more worthy of a hospital visit than his own injury. His thought was interrupted by the realisation that he should call his mother to let her know that he would be delayed, but realised that his phone was probably in a foot-well somewhere in his vehicle.

"Can I get out and retrieve my things?"

The question was aimed at the ambulance guy who had patched him up, but the reply was emitted by his female companion who had escorted the other casualty to the ambulance.

"Yes, but we'll need to get you both off to the hospital. The police are asking for everybody's name and address, so let them know that you're being taken to A&E and they can follow up with you later. Don't worry about collecting your vehicle; they'll move it to a compound for you and you can liaise with your insurance company."

Colin received the instruction and proceeded to squeeze past the other occupants to retrieve his possessions. In doing so he was intercepted by a young policeman who enquired which vehicle was his. Colin indicated towards his blue Ford, that he now realised had been more badly damaged than he had first realised. The front nearside wing and door were heavily distorted, as was the bonnet. The windscreen had been cracked and he was missing both door mirrors. His front right wing and door were also dented following their contact with the dark green car on the other side of the road. Bizarrely, all his lights were still on but the engine had naturally stalled.

"That's mine," he said, "but I have to be ferried to the hospital by the ambulance."

"Fine, but I'll need your details."

Colin took a pen from his inside pocket and a business card from his wallet and proceeded to put his name, address and vehicle registration number on the blank reverse. He handed it to the officer and was expecting to be delayed by the need for a statement, but no request was forthcoming and so he opened his car door and fumbled around for his phone, notepad and strangely, his empty lunch box.

All items were retrieved and so Colin returned to the ambulance. By now it had its engine idling and that perhaps indicated that Colin's brief excursion had delayed everybody. He crept into the awaiting vehicle, the door was closed and they were on their way.

CHAPTER EIGHT
Hidden Gems

Over a week had passed since Colin's accident. He had been forced to take two weeks sick leave as a precaution, as although his trip to the local A&E had not provided any cause for concern, he nevertheless had been instructed to take two weeks off by his line manager. He had nothing to show for his troubles, apart from a slightly sore right ear, and a rather unattractive replacement vehicle that sat on the driveway.

As with most insurance policies, the provision of a replacement vehicle when an accident occurs is normally confined to the cheapest make and model that is on the market at the time. Currently that vehicle was a three-door red Nissan Micra, which was about half the size of the Ford that Colin was used to. However, as he wasn't at work, he didn't really have the time to explore the benefits of such a vehicle. Instead he chose to use his time to catch up with writing various reports on the cases he was engaged on, and helping his mother with odd chores around the house.

Today was a chore day, and Colin had taken it upon himself to rummage through the numerous boxes hidden under beds, in cupboards and under the stairs. He surmised that most of them contained old bank and credit card statements, that could easily be shredded and disposed of, or old magazine articles which had long been overtaken by more modern concepts.

A couple of days previously he had delved under his own bed and retrieved several boxes of old car magazines, football shirts and unwanted gifts. There were several decades of accumulated material as Colin had never moved away from the house, apart from a three-year stay at Durham University. Consequently, much of the stuff that had been squatting under his bed probably hadn't been viewed since.

His memory was jolted back in time as he surveyed various car magazines, each proudly displaying upcoming new vehicles from the manufacturers of the day. There were Triumphs, British Leyland makes of various sizes and more exotic offerings from sleek Italian designers. He actually spent far too long surveying his collection and wondered what to do with them; a charity shop might take them and sell them on as a job lot to an enthusiast, or he could just put them in the recycling. He would have to toss a coin.

The various old clothes were destined for the charity shop, as even if they couldn't sell them as items to wear, they could always be sold on as mixed rag to the industry recyclers. That just left the numerous unwanted gifts that presumably had been kicked under the bed when their usefulness had been discontinued. Most were still boxed, so again the charity shop was a likely exit route for those items.

Today was 'under the stairs day', and Colin set about the task of ducking and crawling into an ever- smaller space where the underside of the foot of the stairs met the floor. The often-used items, such as brooms, mops and vacuum cleaners, were all immediately reachable inside the door. But in the dark recesses were boxes and bags containing odd scraps of material; curtains, part used balls of wool and several boxes of Christmas decorations. Colin had seen these all before, each December when he had been tasked with putting up the festive display, which didn't change from year to year, but behind those items were gems yet to be discovered.

He consequently collected the items he knew about and placed them in the hall whilst he tackled the furthest boundaries with the aid of a torch, which had been conveniently hanging on a hook inside the darkness. Colin had never had to venture this far into the under-stair cupboard, probably not since he was five or six years old when playing hide and seek with his friends. The Christmas decoration boxes were the furthest he ever had to explore, and even that was only an annual visit, so this adventure opened up a new vista for him.

He was confronted with seven medium and small sized brown cardboard boxes. A few were plain, but there were a couple that were presumably from a local grocers or butchers, as they were printed with local names that he knew of, such as Hazelton Butchers, who were still in the High Street, and Frogmore Grocers, whom he couldn't recall, but he did think that he went to primary school with a Donald Frogmore; you don't forget a playground name like that.

He chose the Frogmore box first and reversed out of the cave-like structure and into the living room at the front of the house. The box wasn't sealed but it did have the benefit of each of the four top flaps being interlinked with each-other, thereby giving it a degree of security and strength.

Colin sat cross-legged on the floor and prepared himself. He flicked open the four flaps with a bit of a struggle and peered inside. His curiosity was met with an array of old publications and knitting patterns. Colin remembered how when he was a child, he always seemed to be wearing something that was homemade, whether it was a scarf, a jumper or a cardigan. His mother was obviously well versed in the art of knitting and Colin had now found her secret formula. He flicked through the various pamphlets, occasionally stopping when he vaguely recognised one of the pieces that were being modelled on the front of the publication. Colin was looking at a fawn jumper, which he was pretty sure he once wore, as the chunky knit pattern brought back memories of cold winter mornings when he would make snowmen and throw snowballs. He could never remember feeling cold, so perhaps his mother's skill had been worthwhile.

Having rummaged around in the box for long enough, he concluded that there was nothing of value worth keeping, and so the whole box and its contents were put to one side and Colin ventured back into the wooden cave under the stairs to hopefully find something more interesting.

This time he reversed with two of the smaller boxes balanced together in his right hand. These were plain brown boxes and again the four top flaps had been interwoven to form a sturdy structure. Neither was particularly heavy and so Colin assumed that they would be crammed with further knitting patterns and old magazines. However, one of the boxes felt a bit wobbly and this was therefore the first of the two that he opened when he returned to the front room carpet.

It contained a silver trophy cup mounted on a traditional black wooden plinth. It was heavily tarnished but Colin rubbed his right shirt sleeve on the cup and it reflected a brighter silver area. He turned the item around and noticed that there was an equally tarnished plate mounted on the plinth. He again used his shirt sleeve to rub the offending area and after a couple of vigorous rubs the plate revealed its secret.

There was a small inscription: 'LILIAN & DAVID SMITH, SUSSEX BALLROOM RUNNERS UP'. There was also the briefest of visible dates inscribed underneath, but for some reason it had become worn and so Colin couldn't decipher the exact details. It was almost as if the assumed date had been inscribed at a later time by a different engraver, and the sharpness of the inscription was therefore lost for ever. It was his mother and father's cup; something he never knew existed, and he certainly didn't know that they were a couple with talents that stretched to county level capabilities. Colin felt compelled to enquire and shouted up the stairs to his mother:

"Mumsie, come here. I've found something!"

There was a muffled reply, that had been filtered through a couple of walls before reaching Colin, but he assumed it was affirmative in its nature. This was accompanied a moment later by the sound of footsteps walking across an upstairs floor and the subsequent descent down the stairs, and after a minute Colin's mother was framed in the door surround with an inquisitive look on her face.

"Here, look at this!" said Colin, as he projected the silver cup towards her from his kneeling position. His mother's eyes took on a happy glint as she peered at the item and reached out to take delivery of it. "Oh yes, your dad and I almost won the whole competition."

"But I didn't even know that you were a dancer!" interjected Colin.

"Yes, your dad and I were pretty good in our day. Of course, I stopped when he went away, it didn't seem right to continue without him as my dancing partner."

Colin felt that he should continue the interaction, but his eyes were drawn to a folded piece of paper that had been obscured at the bottom of the box when the flaps fell back into their pre-ordained position. The box must have been static for several decades and so the flaps had naturally folded back into their 'muscle memory' stance; all except one of the shorter sides that remained slightly ajar, and which provided Colin with the view of the paper. He carefully realigned the box flaps allowing the box to breathe again and reached inside to retrieve the item. It appeared to be a couple of pieces of writing paper that had been folded in a natural manner, so as to presumably fit into an envelope. The envelope wasn't in situ but the paper held a compulsion for Colin to open and read the contents. However, as his mother continued to admire the silver cup that she was holding lovingly in her hands, Colin thought that this might be a private letter associated with his father and that perhaps he shouldn't proceed.

He glanced up at his mother, with an expression that seemed to be asking for permission to open the folded item that by now was in Colin's right hand, but which was hidden from his mother's view by the box itself. There was no such permission granted as his mother's attention was still firmly fixed on the cup, and she began to sway to imaginary music, as if recalling the steps that were now playing through her body. Colin therefore thought it wise not to pursue his quest and so let his mother relive a proud moment in her history. He therefore carefully placed the letter back into the box and hoped that his mother would notice it when she eventually finished dancing in her head and replaced the cup back into the cardboard enclosure. His wishes were short-lived as his mother finally broke free:

"I think I should put this on the mantelpiece."

Colin was both disappointed and surprised in equal measures. The cup had been dormant for decades and he could only imagine that his mother's recollection of happier times had now encouraged her to be positive about life. Colin could only support her in her wishes but he really wanted the opportunity to read the letter.

"Good idea Mumsie! There's a space on the left that you could use if you rearrange the area slightly."

His mother danced her way over to the mantelpiece with the music still playing in her head and began allocating space to the various items already in situ. There was a vase from Majorca proudly declaring its position currently in the centre, together with a small green glass miniature bowl that lay to its left. On the right stood a tea light holder in the shape of a lighthouse and a small metal trinket box that contained useful everyday items, such as paper clips, sewing needles and bizarrely, cough sweets. They were quickly rearranged to give the cup pride of place in the centre. His mother stepped back to admire the scenario.

"But it needs a good clean!" she remarked, and quickly retrieved the cup and journeyed to the kitchen to carry out some restoration work.

Colin was now alone in the room. He thought now would be his chance to retrieve the letter and quickly have a read. His mother would be in the kitchen for several minutes, firstly looking for the silver cleaning cloth, which was doubtless at the back of a kitchen cabinet where most little-used items congregate. Then she would spend several minutes rubbing and admiring the ever-shinier cup as she removed decades of tarnish.

He dived into the box and took the letter in his right hand and carefully unfolded the paper and turned it the right way up. It was a letter and it became apparent that it was from his father; well, the person he had always thought was his father. The address at the top left-hand side was a military base somewhere in the world, which Colin couldn't immediately ascertain exactly where, but that was of a secondary nature as he began to read the contents:

Dearest Lilian
I do hope that this letter finds its way to you. Your mother wouldn't give me your new address but said that she would pass it on if I sent it to her – I hope she lets you read it. She said that you were in digs in Western Road. I hope you are okay. I am desperately sorry that we have parted and I would do anything to get you back. I am sorry for what I did; please forgive me. My address is at the top of the letter. Please write back and let me know if you are okay and please, please, forgive me. I will be allowed back on leave in September. If you write back, perhaps we can start again. If I don't hear from you again then my heart will never mend and I will have to accept that my stupid actions have cost me the only woman I have ever loved.
I will love you always. David XXX

Luckily the handwriting was clear and legible and this gave Colin the chance to read the letter again. He had merely scanned it quickly and so a second viewing would hopefully allow him to understand what was admittedly a short letter, but which was obviously profound.

He managed to read it again before he heard his mother shuffling towards him from the kitchen. He hurriedly returned the letter to the box and awaited her arrival. He didn't know what to do or what to say and luckily his mother took the lead by entering the room and declaring:

"There, that looks much better!" and she held out the now gleaming cup in the air in triumph. Colin assumed that she was just admiring her recent handiwork but she could have been reliving the original presentation of the cup.

"Very good!" he responded, with an equal degree of enthusiasm.

Luckily this took the conversation off in a different direction and Colin wouldn't have to remain in the era of his father's letter.

"Yes, it's brilliant," said his mother, who by now had passed Colin's kneeling position and was busy dedicating the new home for the cup on the mantelpiece.

Colin felt obliged not to interrupt what was obviously a proud moment for his mother. He therefore tried to remain normalised, despite his inner desire to ask numerous questions about his father's departure and the reasons for their separation. By inference, it appeared that his father was at fault due to the apologetic nature of the tone in his writings. But there-again the writer of the letter wasn't actually his father, as he had learnt several weeks previously, so perhaps his find wasn't so important after all, although there was something familiar about the contents that bugged him and which he needed to store at the back of his mind for a later time, for now it was time to support his mother.

"Yes Mumsie, that looks great…"

The pair stared at the gleaming cup which was now firmly out of hibernation. His mother's sigh was a clue for Colin to remain quietly kneeling on the floor whilst she fully embraced the moment. Colin couldn't seriously say that his mother was fifty years younger, but for a few minutes she had indeed experienced time travel.

Whilst his mother continued to gaze into the past, Colin quickly unfolded the flaps on the other box and was half expecting to find further objects of mystery, but the only mystery was why someone would want to keep myriad offcuts of wool of all hues, as that was all that resided inside.

"Right," said Colin, getting to an upright position, "I must continue my work."

He retrieved the boxes from the floor and retired to the under-stair cupboard for more exploratory work. His short journey was accompanied by the groan of a man in his fifties extracting himself from an unnaturally long kneeling position, and then finding himself almost in the same position moments later when potholing under the stairs.

He placed the recently viewed boxes to his left side and delved ahead to the next cardboard enclosure. This was a slightly smaller box which had been wedged into the angle at the far end. It wasn't heavy, or particularly light, but Colin felt obliged to explore its contents and so he reversed out from the enclosure and proceeded to return to the living room. His mother had by now retreated to the kitchen and bellowed with a new vigour:

"Do you want a cuppa?"

Colin replied with an equally loud "Yes!"

He gave his mother the benefit of the doubt and assumed that she had imagined his head still being in the far end of the under-stair cupboard. He opened the four flaps of the box whilst awaiting the retreat of the kettle steaming. Again, there was a collection of knitting patterns from a bygone age, some wool but also a small envelope. It had 'Lilian Smith' on the front written in dark blue ink.

To open or not to open, that is the question, thought Colin to himself. The sound of the kettle subsided and Colin tried to calculate how long he would have between the pouring of boiling water over the teabag, the associated brewing, and the arrival of his tea in the front room. Probably a minute at most, and so he quickly turned over the envelope and released the contents. It was a small handwritten note with neat writing which declared:

Dear Lilian Smith
I am so sorry for what happened. I hope you can forgive.
Please accept the enclosed. Please don't tell anyone.

Colin quickly returned the note to its rightful place and put the item back in the box, as by now he could hear his mother approaching from the kitchen.

"Tea," said his mother, volunteering the mug but indicating with her eyes that she would place it on the small table next to the armchair that Colin normally sat in.

Colin got up from the floor and positioned himself accordingly, letting out a satisfying groan as his body finally met with something soft and supportive. It was difficult for him to concentrate on anything other than the words that he had just uncovered; sorry, forgive, recompense and the associated secrecy. He had to quickly think of something to take his mind away from his recent journey into the unknown.

"I should be back at work on Monday," he said, with a degree of inevitability. Even though he was only halfway through his designated period of sick leave, he thought it unfair to continue with housekeeping when he was perfectly capable of being back at work. He felt no pain and was only hesitant about returning to work as he would have to drive something that he didn't really want to drive.

"It's been nice having you around these last few days," replied his mother, who had affixed her gaze back towards the trophy on the mantelpiece.

"Yes, indeed it has," responded Colin, expecting his mother to turn in his direction but she was now five decades away from where he was. Colin consequently finished his tea, got up from his chair, and attempted to return the box to the under-stair cupboard.

He crouched down in the hallway and pushed the box to the back of the dark wedge that obviously hid the odd mystery. He wouldn't dwell on what he had found but he could be safe in the knowledge that he could retrieve the item at will. His mother would not attempt to double herself over to get into the small space, so Colin felt comfortable in letting the matter rest. She didn't know that he had seen the note, and she didn't need to know; she had doubtless forgotten it existed and so there was no incentive to approach the matter… but it would remain at the back of Colin's mind for some time.

CHAPTER NINE
Return of the Jack

Colin pulled up outside Josie's house, and as normal parked as close as he could so that Sam could be aware of his arrival. It was his first day back at work following his accident and Sam was his first port of call. Colin noted that Josie had already opened the front door; her half-frame was just visible through the gap which the open door provided. He wasn't too sure whether something had gone wrong, and Josie was eager to intercept him, or whether she was just concerned that he was okay after his absence.

He realised that Sam hadn't been visited for nearly two weeks and consequently there was an element of guilt that Josie had been stranded for that period. He would have answered the phone if Josie had called him, but protocol dictated that if he was off sick, then off sick he was, and that he shouldn't be proactive from his bed or from wherever else he was recovering. Colin didn't understand this rule as he was perfectly capable of working from home, but those were the restrictions that he had found himself bound by. He had obeyed them up to the point of convincing his line manager that he could return to work earlier than originally planned. Consequently, his journey from his car to the front door was one of curiosity – how had things been during his absence? Was he missed by Sam and had things changed?

"Hiya," was the sound from behind the door, as although Colin couldn't see Josie because of the angle of his approach along the path, she was obviously aware of his impending footsteps. Her greeting was followed by her widening the door opening and the two were soon face to face. Both smiled.

"How are you?" she enquired, with a look of genuine concern on her face, and she ushered Colin into the front room so that they could speak about their recent lives. She indicated for Colin to sit down in the armchair and Josie sat on the sofa.

"I'm fine, thanks. I think they just kept me off as a precaution but my car is in need of more treatment than me. I've come back early as I'm perfectly okay," Colin replied, in a jovial manner trying to set the tone for the day.

"Oh good," replied Josie, lifting the concern from her face, "I noticed that you have a new car."

"Yes, one of those little replacement cars that the insurance companies dish out. Not my choice, I'm afraid!"

Both chuckled in unison, their brown eyes also matching the laughter. Colin continued:

"So, how has your dad been during the last two weeks? I'm sorry that we didn't send anybody else over to support you but we like to try and keep the continuity in these cases; introducing a new person to your father may have been a negative product."

"Oh, that's okay, I understand. He's been a bit miserable – I think he secretly looked forward to your visits, probably because of the blue car that you were driving. I'm not sure what he will say now that you have had to change it…"

Josie was interrupted by Colin remembering that he had

asked her to find out about Uncle Jack's change of car.

"Did you manage to contact your grandfather about when Uncle Jack had his red car? I thought that might help us pinpoint where your father's mind was."

"Yes," continued Josie, "he had to phone me back after he'd rummaged around in some old family photographs that he took with him to Florida, but he reckons that Uncle Jack had the car when dad was about fifteen, and that he had it for about two or three years. So, I assume dad is somewhere between fifteen and eighteen."

Colin became excited by the news but felt compelled to follow up on the accuracy of the information that she had gleaned.

"So, were there any physical aspects that would confirm those ages? I'm thinking photos where the car was at a sports event that could be verified, or at a wedding, christening, that sort of thing?"

"Actually, the car was used at a wedding. There is apparently a photo of the car bedecked with wedding ribbons when it was used for a friend's wedding. Grandad recalls that it was a big celebration as the cricket team had just celebrated winning the national championship; I think he said Surrey, or maybe Sussex, but either way that pinpointed the year and the month, so we know that dad would have been sixteen or possibly seventeen when that photo was taken. Do you think that is where he is now?"

There was a sense of pleading in her voice, as by inference there was hope that Josie's father had been recalled from his early teens and was now residing a further five or so years nearer to her in today. If so, then that implied some form of reversal in his condition. Colin composed himself before volunteering his thoughts:

"Well, I don't want to give any false hope but normally your dad would be retreating further into the past. If he thinks he was twelve years old when I first saw him, it wouldn't be unusual for him to be at ten years old in his mind now. But if he is having memory experiences of when he was sixteen, then that does imply that his journey back in time may be more fluid than we would normally expect. I don't want you to think that his mind will be back to the present day this time next year, as the disease will eventually take him, but it may be a slower journey and maybe, if we can arrange to introduce memories of when he was, say twenty, then we may be able to control his destiny more comfortably."

Josie looked somewhat strained at the thought that her father may be with her for longer than anticipated. There was a part of her that had accepted, and was prepared for, the fact that he would be dead within the year. The new theory that Colin was presenting gave the possibility that her father's life could be elongated. The guilt of perhaps not actually wanting that was something she would have to keep hidden deep inside her.

"Oh, that's good," she said, in a slightly unconvincing way.

Colin took the hint that perhaps this part of the conversation should be concluded and so he raised himself from his sitting position, headed towards the hallway and remarked:

"Right, let's see if we can continue with the process."

He climbed the stairs, leaving Josie with her new-found guilt, and within a few strides he had turned the corner of the landing, knocked on Sam's door and entered into the room. He was greeted with an unexpected salvo of emotion.

"Uncle Jack, you're back!" were the excited words that emanated from an unusually buoyant Sam.

Colin didn't know what to expect after two weeks away from this case, but it certainly wasn't such a change in expression, nor miraculously that he had himself changed from plain old Colin Smith to an Uncle Jack of five decades ago. He consequently stumbled into his opening sentence:

"Yes, yes, I am back."

"I thought you had abandoned me but you're back!"

Not only was there more purpose to Sam's words and diction, there was also more confidence in what he was saying. He definitely wasn't ten or twelve years old anymore; he had grown up. A man in his seventies was now truly a man in his mid-teens. Colin continued the exchange:

"No, I wouldn't abandon you Sam, you know that."

It was difficult for Colin to know how to dictate the conversation. He didn't want to shut off the torrent of words by asking a question that could halt the whole process, so he mused that it would be best to agree or acknowledge what Sam was saying and just let the process take its natural course. He was used to Sam just shutting down the dialogue without reason, so Colin decided that he should just let the whole event flow to whatever conclusion would be available.

"I'm so glad you're back. Dad said that he'd chucked you out. I thought that was wrong and so I was worried that I was left to fend for myself... but you're back! Do mum and dad know you are back?"

That was a tricky one for Colin to muster a quick reply to. He knew from Josie's grandad that Uncle Jack had been a bad influence and that he had been kicked out of the house. The grandfather had said that he was allowed back in and so this must be one of those occasions. Colin didn't know whether to say 'yes' or 'maybe', as whichever answer he gave may have conflicted with history.

"Yes, they do," was the verbal toss of the coin that Colin chose, not knowing whether he had altered history or confirmed it.

"Have they forgiven us?" responded Sam.

Again, it was difficult for Colin to know which direction he should take. On the basis that forgiveness was always preferable, he decided to be affirmative and positive.

"Yes, they are okay with us."

Colin had picked up on the dialogue that Sam was implying. He was no longer alone and they were now a couple, who had both apparently been forgiven, but what Colin didn't know is what had instigated the situation. Why had Sam been so forthcoming and what had they both done to warrant forgiveness? Colin thought quickly about what he had been told, but all he could recall was that Uncle Jack had attacked the lodger and been kicked out of the house. He had been out drinking with Sam at the time of the incident, so the 'us' that Sam referred to probably pinpointed the location where Sam was currently living in his head.

"I didn't think that they would, so it's great that you are back!" continued Sam.

Colin felt obliged to maintain momentum but he was struggling to think of how the conversation should flow. He remembered that Sam got his own car about now and he therefore hesitantly thought about lobbing that subject into the room.

"Have you thought about getting a car?" was as innocent a query as he could manage.

"Yes, Michael's dad said he could get me something, and I've driven a few of his cars around his yard.

We could go out together again."

There was almost a sense of pleading in Sam's voice, as if he felt he should celebrate Uncle Jack's return and repay him for visiting, but as quickly as Sam had volunteered all this dialogue, Colin knew that at some point the banter would arrive at an abrupt stop. That abrupt stop was just a few seconds away.

"Yes, I'd like that," responded Colin.

"You've got a new car. I liked the blue Ford. I don't like the red one you've got."

And those were the last words that would be exchanged that day, as like a switch being flicked, the vague animation and enthusiasm which Sam had displayed suddenly disappeared, and the gaunt, vacant expression returned to haunt the room. Colin knew that was his clue to depart. His experience had told him that once this stage had been reached there was no point in continuing the exchange. The money had run out and the claw had returned to sleep mode.

Josie had presumably heard the vibrant exchange and the subsequent silence. Consequently, by the time Colin reached the bottom of the stairs she was already waiting for an update. She ushered Colin into the living room so that he could impart the news.

"That sounded interesting…I wasn't listening you understand, but I could hear ongoing mumbling, so I assume something happened up there."

"Yes, I don't know what really happened to be honest!"

Where there had been curiosity and apology in Josie's voice, Colin could only respond with a befuddled response but he nevertheless tried to explain:

"I think your father thinks I am Uncle Jack. It may be that the accident which kept me away has mirrored with a point in his life when he was a teenager, and he has just latched onto Uncle Jack's absence and my own and connected the two together. Either way, he's been opening up. What I don't really understand is why he thinks that both he and Uncle Jack need to be forgiven by your grandparents. Unless Sam thinks he is guilty by association; I understand they both went out drinking and…and as a result Uncle Jack was kicked out by your grandmother."

Colin had to be careful, as he couldn't recall whether Josie knew that Uncle Jack had been kicked out for attacking the lodger who was in the house at the time, so he hoped that the drinking incident would suffice. He didn't want to divulge a family secret to her, that her grandfather had deliberately tried to keep secret. Josie didn't respond so Colin thought that she either didn't know the full story, or she had forgotten it. He continued with is thoughts:

"It may have something to do with my replacement car… your father noticed it and said how he liked the old blue Ford better. I'm surmising that perhaps Uncle Jack drove his red car when he returned to visit your father one day and that is where he is in his mind."

"So, you think that dad is getting better?" responded Josie in a hesitantly pleading manner.

"Not exactly, it may just be that your dad's mind has the ability to wander a bit rather than retreat on a pre-determined course. I've not come across it before but I suppose it's possible – I'm sure I've read something about fluidity cases but never exactly experienced one myself. I'll have a rummage around in some manuals and see if I can get some clues as to what may be going on in your dad's mind. But please don't think that your dad is on a road to recovery. He is still going to deteriorate."

Josie again tried to hide her hope that this chapter of her life would soon be over. She was in a difficult mental zone. Her natural love for her father was countered by a willingness to escape the ongoing nightmare of his demise and the frustrations and anger that she had been feeling herself. She also wished for the suffering to stop, but she didn't want to explore whether she wished her own suffering to end and that her father's suffering had become a secondary consideration. She hoped that her facial expressions hadn't conveyed such a message. Luckily Colin understood the pressures that families experience in such situations and he wasn't going to be judge and jury; he just needed to ease Josie and her father through the process that would inevitably end with the death of a loved one. He picked up on her confused expression and so continued with his thoughts:

"I know you want this to end in a timely manner, so let's see if we can make it as comfortable as possible."

That seemed to satisfy Josie, as her face returned to a more normal mode. She appreciated what Colin was trying to achieve and was grateful that there was professional help being offered by him, but deep inside her soul, her desire for her father to die had risen to the top of the agenda.

"I know, I know, and I appreciate you spending the time with dad."

"Thank you, but it's just my job," responded Colin.

With that exchange of words, Colin turned towards the hallway and the door. Josie followed in close formation as Colin reached for the door handle and opened the door towards him to enable his exit. He turned to smile and wave good-bye to Josie, whose head was now protruding from the door frame as if trying to accelerate the leaving process. She preferred to be alone with her guilt.

Colin walked up the path to his parked car and reached into his pocket to retrieve the keys. He pressed the appropriate button on the fob and this was mirrored by a flash of the indicators to acknowledge that access would be permitted.

He opened the driver's door and slid into his seat, glanced up at the bedroom window and noticed that Sam was staring at him. Was that the slightest of smiles on Sam's face? Colin smiled back but couldn't be certain if he was imagining an exchange of expressions. He would have to await his next visit to see if new ground had been broken.

It was later that day when Colin pulled into his driveway. He could see that his mother had already opened the front door to allow him easier access to the house. She may have noticed that he had not added his house key to the fob which held his hire car key, and therefore her action may have precluded a fumble or juggle in the driveway as the correct key was found from a different pocket.

There was something about driving a hire car that had a naturally temporary feel about it; the car was only to be with him for a short while, whereas the house would hopefully be with him forever, or at least until he chose to change locations.

The hire car wouldn't have been personalised with his own possessions; it would remain virtually as when it was handed over to him, and therefore Colin didn't feel obliged to add his own touches to the experience. No air freshener hanging from the interior mirror, no stickers on the back window alerting other road users to his preference of football club, nor any witty comments about the politicians of the day. He therefore chose not to introduce the two keys to each other, probably for fear of some unknown contamination that could result in the two keys formally being introduced.

As it was his first day out of the house it was probably a wise move by his mother. There was a temptingly placed drain mid-route between the parking area and the front door that was just begging to be the subject of a catastrophe, as one or both keys could somehow be magnetised towards the floor if Colin had attempted to find the required key from his pockets. It would surely happen one day as he always had one arm occupied with his case and the other with his car key. The introduction of a third item would naturally require one item to be likely dropped. Colin was therefore free to meander to the front door without the need for any drama, and he casually hit the lock button on the key fob, which alerted the neighbours to his return by a somewhat overloud toot.

"Hello, how was your first day?" enquired his mother, who was now standing in the doorway.

"Good enough to celebrate with a cup of tea and a biscuit," responded Colin with a cheery tone to his voice.

"Dinner won't be long but I suppose you could have a cup of tea and a biscuit, seeing as it's your first day back!"

The exchange was complete and Colin and his mother went

their separate ways, with Colin collapsing into an armchair in the living room and his mother continuing into the kitchen to carry out the immediate task of refreshment. The door somehow knew that it was time to close but his mother's gentle nudge gave it the clue. The working world was now outside, to be re-visited the following day and both could now relax. Except that Colin had promised to try and find some journals on the fluidity of memory in patients such as Sam, and so his rest would be a temporary one.

"Do you know where I put the medical journals and papers that I had from a couple of years ago?" shouted Colin to his mother, who luckily hadn't put the kettle on yet and so she could reply relatively easily:

"Under the stairs, I think. Didn't you come across them the other day?" was the slightly reassuring response from his mother.

"I didn't get to go through all the boxes, so I know there are a couple still to be looked at."

The latter few words had to be shouted, as by now the kettle had indeed started to boil and Colin assumed that his mother had heard. She surely had, as a couple of minutes later she came into the room armed with a mug of tea, a small plate of chocolate biscuits and the words: "Well I'm sure it can wait until after dinner."

Colin nodded, as he had already taken a bite out of a biscuit as she finished her sentence. The tea was balanced in his other hand, ready for a slurp, but was too hot to instigate that move, and so a further bite from the biscuit finished off the initial member of the trio which had been residing on the plate. His mother turned around to complete the preparation of the dinner, which in reality only required the contents of the oven to be emptied onto two plates, but she felt obliged to leave her son to enjoy his refreshment in peace. He completed the task of biscuit removal with minimum effort.

"Ah, that's better," Colin muttered to himself, as he finally took a gulp of tea. His mother had put just the right amount of milk into the mug to enable him to overcome the heat of the liquid. The three biscuits task had occupied the time necessary to allow an adequate cooling of the recipe. In a further minute the tea had joined the biscuits. All was well.

Colin's mother must have been aware of the progress, as she had soon returned with a tray, on which had been placed a plate of inviting homemade lasagne and an accompaniment of garlic bread.

"Now don't you let me down – don't let the biscuits get in the way of eating this!" said his mother with a wry smile on her face. She knew from experience that Colin would have no trouble in completing the task in hand.

"Lovely!" responded Colin, from an anticipatory sitting position that had changed from the relaxed laid-back situation of tea and biscuits.

Whilst lasagne wasn't necessarily his most favourite of meals, anything that his mother had made from scratch was always welcome. As his mother returned to the kitchen to collect her own serving, Colin merrily tucked into the contents on his plate. It was obvious that his mother's cooking had helped to cement their relationship over the decades. She had always been a great cook and Colin hoped that she always would be. It wasn't a surprise therefore, that by the time his mother had returned and adjusted her seating position to begin her own task, Colin had nearly completed his own consumption and was busily trying to mop up the last cheesy juices with a piece of garlic bread.

"Ooh, that was good!" he exclaimed.

"I suppose you want some of mine, do you?" was the obvious response, as his mother held her first fork of lasagne to her mouth. "I've left some in the kitchen. Go on, help yourself!"

Colin had anticipated that there should be a spare portion somewhere. He knew the size of the lasagne dish, and history had taught him that he either was presented with a very large plate of lasagne, or there would be an additional smaller portion still in the dish somewhere in the kitchen. He consequently didn't need a second invitation to remove himself from his chair and take the short journey to where his second helping would presumably be waiting for him.

"Great!" he said in anticipation of the offer, and he was soon back in his chair demolishing the remaining contents of his mother's hard work.

His mother smiled with a sense of pride, not in her own handiwork, but that she had brought up such a grateful and loving son on her own. He still loved her and she still loved him.

Colin must have been hungry, as he was only just finishing his final mouthful of his second helping as his mother was finishing her own first plateful.

"Dessert?" she enquired.

"Mmm!" murmured Colin, with an accompanying nod, as his mouth was still full of lasagne.

His mother slowly raised herself from her chair and proceeded back towards the kitchen. Colin noticed that whilst she still had all her faculties, she was getting to the age where movements from a sitting position were taking longer, and whereas he could leap up from his chair, his mother would have to think about extracting herself from such a scenario. Her initial movements were slower, but once she was up, momentum probably took over until her regular stride was allowed to intercept the process.

Lasagne was concluded, and Colin continued to chew the final mouthful as he followed his mother into the kitchen to return his tray and plate.

"Lovely. Thanks Mumsie," he said, as the pair jostled for position. The kitchen wasn't small but if two people wanted to do the same thing at the same time, then invariably there would be a traffic jam. Both were trying to put their plates and cutlery into the sink, which was only one person's width in diameter. Naturally, Colin took his turn behind his mother, who then moved towards the fridge to retrieve the prepared dessert. Colin guessed that it would be a home-made trifle, which his mother was particularly good at making, but at the same time he would be pleased with anything that she had taken the trouble to make.

"Go and sit down," said his mother and Colin duly obliged, but in walking back to the front room he carefully flicked the toggle catch on the under stairs cupboard door so that it swung open a little. This was to remind him to try and find his old notes in one of the boxes that were inside.

He often left things slightly untidy. He would drop the garden shed keys on the floor by the door to the rear garden, or throw his cheque book onto an otherwise empty table, to remind him to do something, namely go to the garden shed for something, or write a cheque to somebody. Somehow the visual jolt was better than trying to remember where he had put a 'to do' list, which invariably he would find three days after he should have done something on the list.

Colin sat down in his chair in anticipation of dessert.

"You know what it is," said his mother with an air of reluctance. It was indeed homemade trifle.

Colin had never asked his mother what made her trifle so much better than anybody else's. It had some form of alcohol in it, probably rum or sherry, but there was also the texture of the custardy topping which was always creamier than it should be. And the strawberries were always fresh, rather than tinned, and the sponge always had a substantial texture, allowing the alcohol and strawberry juices to be fully absorbed without making the whole thing too soggy. It was the best. His mother was the best too.

The portion his mother had given him was definitely about correct in size. He could manage this without feeling bloated. He would be satisfied on two counts; he would not need to undo his trousers a notch to accommodate his recent meal and secondly, he knew there would be some left for tomorrow. When he had finished the bowl of trifle, he would therefore decline any offer of a second portion and would await a repeat performance the following day. His mother returned to the front room and smiled, as she knew exactly what her son was thinking.

"There is always tomorrow," she remarked, as she took her seat.

Colin nodded in agreement and allowed her to finish her meal. He returned to relax mode by adjusting his position in his chair to allow his meal to complete its journey. He closed his eyes and let his thoughts wander; the only slight interruption was the occasional gentle tap of his mother's spoon against her china bowl, which started to have a regular beat to it, and which he tried to match to a song he knew. Nothing materialised, and so Colin just continued to rest, allowing whatever was around him to fade into the background. He didn't notice that his mother had finished her trifle, or that she had got up and proceeded to the kitchen to do the washing up. Colin had nodded off.

His mother loved him dearly but as she had exited the front room, she noticed the under stairs cupboard was slightly ajar, and realised that Colin had set a reminder for himself; to do something involving crawling under the stairs again to retrieve the papers he had mentioned earlier. His habit of leaving things untidy, or out of place, was the one aspect that she frowned upon.

She had been brought up to keep everything neat and tidy; a door that was ajar, or keys left in the middle of a hallway, were not in keeping with her strict tidiness regime. That had been the only matter that had caused any anguish up until recently, when Colin had forced her to reveal the details of his ancestry. Having kept that matter dormant for many decades, the recent realisation that Colin now knew of her past had caused her a lot of internal pain and soul searching. As that subject had now been brought to the foreground, perhaps she was more accepting of the cupboard door being ajar. Previously she may have nudged it closed again but that aspect seemed secondary today, and she proceeded to do her chores in the kitchen without feeling the need to correct anything.

Unfortunately, with her desire to complete the washing up with the minimum of noise, the Law of Sod decided to intervene.

Whilst she was busy thinking of the past, the present decided to remind her that soapy hands and equally soapy plates do not have a force of attraction when the mind of the holder is not in the kitchen too. There was an exceptionally loud clatter as the dinner plate she had been holding suddenly slipped from her hands and crashed to the hard floor, consequently breaking into several large pieces and awakening both her and Colin, who in unison cried out.

"You alright Mumsie?" blurted Colin, as he simultaneously awoke, spoke, leapt and trotted at the same time, and before the question mark in his statement had ended his shout, he was in the kitchen and on his knees picking up the remnants of the plate that he could see.

"Sorry son!" she exclaimed, with a slightly nervous apprehension in her voice. She was aware that she had journeyed into the past but didn't want that to be known, as it would only invite Colin to ask some more awkward questions, so she continued with an often-used explanation:

"It's my age, dear!"

Colin didn't argue but continued to assemble the pieces of the plate into their rough formation before volunteering to get the hoover from under the stairs to complete the task.

"Don't move," he said, as he recoiled from his kneeling position and went to the under stairs cupboard to get the hoover. He noticed that the cupboard door was still ajar, and that reminded him that he would have to be on all fours again shortly to carry out a task for his work.

"Coming!" he said, as he plugged one end of the attached wire to an electrical socket in the hallway, whilst simultaneously unwinding the coiled cable with his other hand. He soon had sufficient cable to carry out the task, and having attained a suitable stance, hit the switch on the handle and proceeded to suck up whatever small pieces of debris were on the floor. He didn't need to speak whilst performing the task; a noisy hoover and a conversation are not possible at the same time, and so having reached a degree of satisfaction, he turned off the machine and uttered the often overused expression: "That's done it!" which seemed to be applicable to any small job that corrects a misdemeanor of life.

His mother turned around and smiled. "Thank you, son."

Colin went to return the hoover to its home, but before inserting it back in its rightful place he thought he'd take the opportunity to retrieve the required box whilst he had the extra bit of wriggle room available, and so crouching down, he entered the under stairs cupboard, switched on the dim torch light and proceeded to have a rummage.

He remembered that he had sorted through a couple of boxes in the deep apex of the cupboard, but there were still several that were virgin. Now on his knees and crouching even further, he proceeded to move the boxes around, and in doing so touched the box that held the mysterious letters he had viewed previously. Curiosity got the better of him, and he carefully opened the offending box again and retrieved the envelope that had intrigued him. He again opened the envelope with a degree of guilt that had multiplied since he last looked at the note. He knew what it had said but he felt compelled to read the note again, as if somebody had added a few more paragraphs during the intervening period. He adjusted the angle of the light.

Dear Lilian Smith
I am so sorry for what happened. I hope you can forgive.
Please accept the enclosed. Please don't tell anyone.

Colin studied the note again. The writing was neat, implying that it had been written by an educated and thoughtful person; it wasn't rushed in format, nor were the letters sloping widely away as if written in a hurry. This was written with some thought attached to it and it also implied some form of payment had been made. 'Hush money,' thought Colin to himself. His imagination went into detective mode as he surmised that this could be a letter written by his mother's attacker… and therefore it could be his actual father's writing too. Half of him wanted to ask his mother about the letter; the other half wanted to hide it again, so that it wouldn't be found until fifty years' time when a new buyer of the house would find it when clearing out the unwanted items.

"Do you want tea?" interrupted Colin's thinking and he turned his head and shouted from the apex:

"Yes please."

That was his clue to replace the letter into the box and retrieve the box that he was actually looking for, and so with a bit of rummaging and groaning, Colin came across a medium-sized box with the words: 'STUFF I'LL NEVER NEED' written on the side in black felt tip. This was obviously the box he wanted, as it reflected his dry sense of humour, which always accompanied a situation where he was asked to keep hold of something that he didn't really want. He was sure there was also a similarly marked box with unwanted Christmas and Birthday presents that old aunts and uncles may have given him. It was probably a very big box.

Having found what he was looking for, he carefully reversed out of the cupboard until he could kneel in an upright position and, leaning on the floor, exited the under stairs cave. He reached in to drag the box and proceeded to return himself to a fully upright position with the box cradled in front of him.

"Have you found it, dear?" said his mother, who whilst she couldn't actually see him due to her back being towards him, judged that by the sounds echoing from under the stairs that he had been successful.

"Yep, got it!" replied Colin, who marched triumphantly to his armchair and sat down.

He placed the box between his legs, which were in the ten to two position, leaned forward and carefully removed some ancient yellowing adhesive tape from the top of the box, which held the two large flaps in place. The fact that this box was secured with tape, as opposed to being secured by merely interlocking the four roof flaps, indicated that this box was of no importance at all. He peered inside and indeed the box contained all the material he had amassed from various conferences on dementia, memory loss, palliative care, psychology and whatever other subject was thought to be of importance by the system that employed him. He rummaged a bit further and retrieved a small folder that had been anointed with his own handwriting. He had taken the time to provide a list of the subject matter which rested inside, and at number six on the list was what he was looking for: 'Non-static memory recall'. He would have to await reading the actual contents as the whole process was interrupted by that often-used excuse – tea!

"Here you are!" muttered his mother, as she handed Colin a mug of tea.

"Thanks Mumsie!" was the natural response that Colin would always respond with, and having mentally stopped for tea, he put the folder back to rest on the top of the box, which had decided that its flaps should return to their natural closed position.

"Have you found what you were looking for?" enquired his mother. "Yep, went straight to it. I'm pretty sure that what I need is in there."

"Oh good, dear," said his mother, with a degree of indifference as she took a sip of tea. Colin did likewise and they both proceeded to drain their receptacles to a natural conclusion. It was therefore some five minutes later when Colin put his empty mug down and returned to the small folder.

He flicked through the myriad of pages, as if looking for a particular slot that he knew existed, and within a few seconds his fingers had stopped at section six.

It wasn't a particularly full section, but it did contain the words of wisdom that confirmed his own thoughts; patients with a particular stage of age-related memory loss had been noted 'living' in eras that covered several years of past experiences. It went on to explain that this condition had limitations and that no case had ever resulted in a cure, whereby the patient returned to today; the suffering just moved around a bit within a pre-determined range of dates, normally instigated by mirroring events of yesterday with similar events of the present. Colin concluded that his theory of his own absence, and the change of car to his current red temporary model, had likely moved Sam a couple of years nearer to him. He realised that there were limitations to what he could achieve, but he mused on the possibility of introducing Sam to his own handwriting of when he was in his late teens or early twenties, to see if that could continue his journey. Sam had obviously been prepared to move a couple of years, so why not take advantage of the momentum? That would be his plan for his next few visits, so he put the folder back in its box and sat back with an air of contentment. He had a plan…and an empty mug.

"Mumsie, any chance of a follow up cuppa?!" was his triumphant request.

"Oh, alright then!" was the affirmative reply from his mother and she duly returned to the kitchen to boil yet another kettle.

Whilst his mother carried out the very important task of refreshment, Colin started the job of returning the box to the cupboard under the stairs. He couldn't be bothered to try and find where the roll of tape was located in the house, or even whether they had such a roll available, so the conclusion was that he would try to fold the four top flaps into a secure position. He had retrieved what he was looking for and now the box should be returned to the bunker.

He crouched down, eventually kneeling and pushed the box into the apex. He could see that there were probably two or three shoeboxes that he hadn't explored recently. One was particularly tempting as the outside image conveyed that a pair of ladies dancing shoes would be inside. There was obviously a temptation to take a look and, whilst he thought about retrieving the contents, he was surprised to notice that the box was restrained by a light blue ribbon that was neatly tied with a bow at the top. This implied one of two things; either the contents were special in some way, or there was a danger that the top of the box would become detached from the main item beneath.

Had he been quicker he could have had a peek inside but the whole process was interrupted by the warm words of his mother: "Tea!"

The shoe box adventure would have to wait for another day.

CHAPTER TEN
Return of the Colin

The day was bright and sunny as Colin parked his car outside of his favourite appointment. Josie had now got into the habit of anticipating his arrival and had left the front door ajar. Having secured his car, Colin journeyed down the path and through the doorframe and into the hallway. A muffled shout of "In here!" greeted his arrival. Colin took the hint and entered the front room. His entry was accompanied by the final death throes of a boiling kettle, and was quickly followed by the arrival of Josie with a mug of something brown and warm in each hand. She thrust one towards him, with the expression of hope that she had remembered what Colin drank and how he liked it. She didn't get to ask for confirmation as Colin took control of the mug.

"Thanks," he said, and positioned himself to sit in the armchair, which seemed to be his domain whenever he visited and there was the need for a chat. Josie was quick to assert herself and it was evident that she had been practising for this moment. She consequently took the lead with her opening question:

"Did you find the paperwork concerning dad's possible condition?"

"Yes, yes, I did – it's as I thought, there can be a degree of fluidity. Actually, I'd like to try an experiment – do you have any of dad's early writing? I'm thinking perhaps from his late teens or early twenties. I appreciate that may be a bit of a tall order. He presumably would have finished schooling at an early age, so any old school reports may be a bit too early, but if you have anything from that period, I would like to try and use it."

Josie looked back at him with a puzzled expression. Colin took the hint to explain further.

"I am thinking that if we can find something that your dad wrote from that sort of period, I might be able to bring him back a bit further. And if that works, then maybe we can keep trying to reverse him out of his teenage years."

Josie looked slightly disappointed but it wasn't evident whether this was because she had her own carefully rehearsed plan knocked off track by Colin's thoughts, or whether it was Colin's actual words that had meant her life of suffering would be stretched out even further than the few months that she had planned for. If her father could be reversed nearer to today, then her estimate of freedom would need to be recalculated.

"Oh, I see," was the best she could respond with.

Luckily, Colin didn't catch her expression and so he continued with the enthusiasm that was becoming proportional to Josie's disappointment:

"Yes, I think it could work – my notes indicated that there was a good chance that we could make some progress. Do you think there is any hope that you could find some of dad's writings?"

Josie was the sort of person who didn't like to offend, or disappoint, and so she nodded with a thoughtful expression, as if she was already searching the attic for boxes of old papers that may be suitable for Colin's purposes. Consequently, she could only offer an affirmative response:

"Yes," was forthcoming from her side of the discussion.

"Great!" said Colin, who took a few further gulps of coffee before indicating that he should perhaps journey upstairs to see his challenge of the day. Josie nodded again and so Colin raised his half empty mug in thanks and entered the hall before mounting the staircase.

Josie remained static. She had planned to make Colin aware that she and Steve were having marital tensions. She had long wanted to start a family but Steve had always refused to engage with her whilst her father was upstairs, as he – probably correctly – thought that she wouldn't be able to cope with both a new born, who would be helpless, and her father who would be just as helpless as time moved forward.

She was going to ask Colin whether he could investigate moving her father out of the house and into a specialist care home. She had hoped that as her father deteriorated back to year zero, any physical move for him would be less stressful if he really didn't know where he was. The fact that he had always lived in the house – and indeed was born in it – had always played on Josie's mind that it would be cruel to move him out. But if he reached the stage where he didn't know that the house he was in had any memories, then she would consider a care home situation. That was what she was going to indicate to Colin but he was on a different journey; one that would make it difficult for her plan to be introduced if her father was going to get better. She and Steve would have to be patient.

Colin reached the top of the stairs and turned towards

Sam's room, knocked on the door as always to indicate that he was about to enter, and continued towards his client.

Sam was sitting upright in bed and averted his gaze away from the window and towards his visitor.

There was a vague recognition but nothing verbal was forthcoming.

"Hello Sam," was the best that Colin could open the batting with.

There was no new response from Sam, which was disappointing as Colin had hoped that they could continue from their last session, but it looked as though it would be a difficult start to the day. Last time he was Uncle Jack and he wondered whether he had now reverted to plain old Colin. Surprisingly, there was delayed recognition as Sam offered a belated response:

"Mum said you'd be coming today but she called you Colin."

Colin had to think quickly, as having prepared himself a second ago to ask some open-ended questions to get the process started, here was the recognition he wanted but unfortunately an awkward question accompanied it.

"Colin is one of my middle names and apparently a person called Jack has moved in next door; I think your mum got confused."

He had no idea what possessed him to introduce a fictional middle name to Sam's uncle, or why he had possibly confused the whole situation by implying that one of the next-door neighbours had moved out, and somebody new – called Jack – had moved in. But that was all that could be summoned from his creative brain at short notice.

There was silence and Colin felt obliged to break it:

"I'm still Uncle Jack," he said nervously, as if trying to bring the train back onto the right track.

Sam didn't have many expressions, but whatever they were, they always held a gaunt background but that gauntness ebbed slightly as he responded:

"No, you're not! You can't be – you've been kicked out and were told never to return!"

Again, this conversation wasn't going according to plan and now there was a degree of hostility to the atmosphere. Colin was aware that people with fading memory and dementia patients could often become violent and abusive, and Colin realised that he may have unlocked that door.

"Why do you say that?" was an obvious response from Colin, hoping to get a degree of companionship back into the exchange.

"You're not him. You don't look like him. You must be that bloke 'Colin' that mum said would be coming but I don't know why you are here; why don't you go?!"

This was a totally unexpected turn in the history of their conversations and Colin realised that his time had probably run out before it had even started, but he asked one final question:

"Sam, how old are you?"

"Why, what's it to you?" was the terse response. "It's important Sam; are you fourteen?"

"No!"

"Sixteen?"

There was no response, but rather than accept that sixteen was Sam's mental age, he ploughed on for some form of positive response:

"Seventeen?"

"Yes, I'm seventeen. Now go!"

Colin had the information he wanted and it was evident that this conversation was now over. He consequently exited the room and slowly trudged downstairs to a waiting Josie, who had been alerted by the unusual raised voice of her father.

"What happened?" was her obvious question as she ushered Colin into the front room once more.

Colin again took up position in the armchair with Josie mirroring his action by sitting opposite him on the sofa.

"He no longer recognised me as Uncle Jack; in fact, I don't think he recognised me at all, so I'm not sure what has sparked the change of attitude. But I did extract that he thinks he's seventeen, which may help. I'd still like you to try and find some of your dad's writings from a similar era, but if we know that he thinks he is seventeen, then anything approaching his twenties, or in his early twenties, would be worth a try. It's not unusual for your dad's condition to make him appear abusive; it just means that he's confused or frustrated, and with me trying to be Uncle Jack, when obviously I am not, has probably tipped the scales this time. I think we were just lucky previously."

Josie held her right hand to her mouth in mock shock. Secretly she realised that maybe her father had reverted to his original journey and that seventeen would be the oldest he would be before continuing back to eventual death. Colin didn't recognise her predicament and Josie didn't think it would be suitable to re-introduce her story of marital problems. Maybe her desire for her father's demise should remain concealed for a bit longer. She tried to continue the conversation along more acceptable lines:

"I thought you were doing so well after the last visit. Do you really think any of his writings will help?"

She was desperately looking for an excuse not to venture into the loft and potentially prolong her discomfort, but unfortunately Colin's response was too keen for her not to try and give ground on this occasion.

"It is worth a try, if only to say that we tried to move your father's mind nearer to us. There is also some scientific knowledge that I should share if we do manage to help your father in this way."

It was evident that Josie would be stuck in a childless world for a bit longer and that her father would still be part of her life; a big part of her life that prevented her from fulfilling her own desires and wishes.

But being the obedient person that she had always been, she agreed that she would try and find some of her father's writings from his early twenties.

"Okay, I'll have a look around tomorrow. I think the loft is the most likely place as everything downstairs was sorted when we decorated a couple of years ago."

"Great! If you find anything give me a call on my mobile so that I can think about preparing a synopsis."

That was the finality which ensured that Josie would indeed be putting on her old clothes and climbing a ladder to a part of the house that she hadn't ventured into for well over a decade. Her husband had been up there a couple of times but she had no idea what could be up there, apart from darkness, cold and dust.

Colin concluded that the end of his visit had arrived and so he positioned to get up from the armchair. Again, Josie mirrored his actions, and the two for a second looked like a pair of mating swans as their torsos wavered together. Colin was the first to break free and proceeded to exit the room towards the front door.

"Bye," he said.

"Bye," Josie repeated.

Colin proceeded towards his car and as always hit the 'open' button on the car key fob, which alerted the vehicle to flash its hazard lights as if greeting his arrival. Opening the door and sliding into the driver's seat, he casually glanced up towards Sam's bedroom window but for once Sam's face was not staring back at him, and whatever bond that the two had cemented last time had truly disappeared. Colin knew from previous cases which he had worked on that this could be a watershed moment; Sam could retreat into his life of a seventeen-year-old, who by now may feel cheated and lied to that Uncle Jack was no longer Uncle Jack. The conduit between the decades had been broken.

On the drive to his office Colin thought hard about the turnaround which he had experienced. His previous visit had been so positive and yet his last hour had been a failure in every sense. Not only had Sam not recognised him, for once he actually questioned and disagreed with him. Apathy had been overtaken only briefly by enthusiasm and now he was faced with slight anger and obstructiveness. But to remain positive, Colin realised that his Uncle Jack impression had arrived without warning and consequently, if he remained positive, perhaps another episode would again bring some degree of progress. If Josie could find some handwriting from her father's early twenties, that might just bring Sam back on track. But he realised that he was perhaps putting too much emphasis on visual stimulants when he already knew that Sam had not recognised photos of himself when he was older. But he would have been a lot older in the wedding photograph that had a broken glass. Perhaps a photo of when he was in his twenties would also help?

It never ceased to amaze Colin that whenever he was driving and thinking deeply about a case, he nevertheless always managed to get to his destination without incident. He could never remember approaching various familiar traffic lights and junctions, but somehow he must have negotiated them in the correct manner. He had never had a camera inspired speeding ticket, or a notice through the post advising him that he had jumped a red light, and this led him to think that perhaps he had two brains; one would be observing and reacting to anything that happened, and the other would be in constant analytical mode, solving problems and thinking obscure deep thoughts. It was therefore no surprise, but with some relief, that Colin approached his office block for a regular monthly visit.

As he turned his car into the car park and lowered his window, he stretched out his hand and carefully entered a four-digit code onto a vertical key pad that was mounted on a pole. The red and white striped barrier, which had temporarily halted his advance, gradually lifted itself into a saluting position and Colin proceeded to the next stage of his day.

He swung the car around to an often-used space which was against a wall. There were plenty of spaces available but familiarity was such that 'his' space was what he wanted, and without an adjacent car to restrict his momentum, the whole manoeuvre was carried out without slowing or changing down a gear.

He sat motionless for a few seconds, thinking about how his connection with Sam had been lost and how all his good work had been undone by a few awkward exchanges. He was now banking on Josie not only finding some familiar writings but also that Sam would recognise and engage with him once more. Those thoughts over, Colin opened the car door, reached down for some papers that were residing in the passenger foot well, and got out of the car and went through the routine of locking it.

He stared up at the ten-storey building that was above him, as if expecting his colleagues to be leaning out of the windows and waving encouragingly, but no such welcome was apparent, probably because the windows didn't open in the airconditioned building, and probably because he was the first to arrive for the meeting. In which case, he would have first dibs on the biscuit selection!

Having smiled at the receptionist when he walked through the revolving doors, he proceeded to the lift lobby and swiped his identity card against a metal pillar, which enabled two small glass screens to part in front of him. He hurried to an awaiting lift, stepped inside and hit button eight. The doors slid together with a satisfying whoosh, and in no time he was propelled upwards and towards his meeting. There was a 'ping' from outside which indicated that floor eight had been achieved, and as the doors parted, again with the whoosh that Colin thought was deliberately set at a level that was calming, he bounded out to his left and through some double doors and into his own reception area.

"Morning Colin!" said the cheery woman sat behind the desk.

"Morning Cindy," replied Colin, trying to match her degree of enthusiasm but probably falling a notch short. She was employed for her pleasant welcoming demeanour and was meant to be inviting and available to assist any person that ventured through the doors. Colin could be enthusiastic and welcoming but not today. He ventured towards the meeting room and as expected, he would be having free reign of the biscuit selection that sat in the middle of the large glass topped table.

There were eight chairs orbiting the biscuits, but none was occupied, and so Colin selected his normal location and pulled back the corresponding chair which allowed him a closer inspection of the biscuit tray's contents, and which also afforded him a view of whatever part of Sussex lay beneath him on the horizon.

He grabbed at an adjacent stack of plates and removed the top one, which was soon full of a selection of mainly chocolate covered delights. He was careful not to take too many of the same style, although he did muse that if he consumed all of the dark chocolate ones before anyone else joined the meeting, then perhaps nobody would notice their absence. He settled for a varied assortment and nibbled his way through his catch.

There was a coffee and tea making machine in the corner of the room. There was also a selection of juices and water, but that pleasure would wait until at least the first plate of biscuits had been disposed of, which as it turned out was considerably quicker than it should have been.

Colin leant forward again and put another four suitably

random biscuits on his plate, placing them well within his own zone of influence. He then got up to retrieve a mug of coffee from the corner of the room. The tea from the machine had always been ghastly and so decaf Columbian was his choice, and as the machine made all sorts of strangulation type noises, he went back to the desk and arranged his papers in a manner that suggested he was more professional than he actually was. Anybody now entering the room couldn't accuse him of only being there for the biscuits.

The machine stopped gasping for help and Colin retrieved his prize and sat down in anticipation of his colleagues joining him. He could hear a commotion behind him, which emanated from the lift lobby area, and it became evident that one of the lifts had dispensed his colleagues onto floor eight, as whatever they were talking about in the lift continued into the lobby and into the meeting room.

"Morning!" said Colin, to the mass of humanity that appeared to tumble into the room, but which somehow had a degree of order, as each member took up a rehearsed position around the table without anybody bumping into each other.

There was a unified "Hello!" from his colleagues, almost as if they had been rehearsing it.

Tom Farr took up position at what was considered the head spot and proceeded to welcome Colin to the meeting. He was younger than Colin by about a decade and had been parachuted in from somewhere when the last restructuring of the unit took place. Colin never did understand why.

Tom didn't need to mention his colleagues as obviously they had all exchanged pleasantries on route. They too were busy helping themselves to the contents of the tray and Colin winced internally as the remaining pile of biscuits got ever smaller. But he was one full plate ahead of everybody else. When they had settled into their chairs, removed whatever clothing they felt necessary, and arranged their papers in front of themselves, Tom opened the day's proceedings.

"Okay everybody, thanks for coming along today. I know it's only once a month that we have these things but I appreciate you all attending. Today's agenda is as follows – 1. A quick run round the team for updates on anything unusual in their cases, 2 – Budgets for next financial year, 3 – Q & A on anything of a wider nature, and 4 – Updates on procedures. Actually, let's have Q & A at the end and move procedures to number three."

All nodded in agreement as they scribbled down the agenda. "Okay, Len you go first."

Len was one of the more experienced members of the team, which was highlighted by the numerous lines etched into his face and the thinning grey hair that implied that he was either very old or had been consumed with worry during a shorter life. He leaned forward in his chair and proceeded to enlighten the room with an interesting case about a violent verbal attack that one of his cases had subjected his son to. The case had been living with dementia for about a decade and it appeared that every exchange of words would now end in a shouting match. Whilst the son had a reasoning filter that he had full control of, the father had no such control and any filter he had, had worn out long ago. The team suggested upping medication.

Lisa, who sat next to Len, merely remarked that all her cases were no different to when they last met. She was a new member of the team and probably still working out the pecking order of the assembled attendees. She consequently turned her gaze to her right, where John was almost exploding with enthusiasm about how he had introduced a client to some photos and writings that they had taken and written when they were younger. And how the patient had improved once he had latched onto a particular photo of a beach holiday which they had had many decades ago. In addition, his case had reacted positively to old music, which matched the era of the photos.

Colin felt slightly deflated, as that was obviously going to be his plan of action with Sam, and which he was going to proudly introduce to the team. However, John had introduced an additional potential trigger; music.

John had always been considered a direct rival to Colin. They were both roughly the same age, with the same level of experience, and Colin always felt that he had come out second-best whenever there was a round-up of cases. He couldn't even console himself that John looked older; he didn't, and so Colin would inevitably feel slightly downbeat whenever the two were in the same room together.

"Yes, I'm about to do that with one of mine," was the best Colin could fabricate.

John, having felt the warm glow of glory, turned to David on his right. He too had nothing much to report and so invited Colin to carry the baton.

"I have this case where I am about to do the same sort of thing as John. The guy is in his seventies but thinks he's seventeen, so I have asked the daughter to try and find some writings from when he was about twenty, just to see if I can move him nearer to today. Unfortunately, this morning whatever connection we had previously was halted and I feel I might have to start again. Hopefully the writings will help."

John made some affirmative sounds whilst consuming a Hob Nob.

Felix, who was sitting adjacent to Colin, then opened up with the news that he too was trying a similar procedure. Again, Colin felt slightly dejected that he was being diluted, so he consoled himself with another biscuit from the tray. He hadn't eaten the four that he had previously selected but he just felt like a further treat.

Alex and Robert had nothing specific to add and so Tom moved the team onto the next subject. Colin had almost switched off in anticipation of the next topic, as budgets were not his thing, and so it was a relief when his mobile rang and he could see that it was Josie calling.

"I'm sorry I have to take this," he said nervously, as he got up from his chair and exited the room to retrieve whatever news was coming his way. Tom nodded affirmatively whilst starting to talk numbers with the rest of the team.

"Hello?" said Colin, from the confines of the carpeted space in between the glass fronted rooms that formed a natural corridor of quietness.

"Hello," said Josie, "sorry to disturb you, can you talk?"

"Yes, you've just got me out of a rather boring office meeting, so take as long as you like!"

Colin tried to inject some humour into the proceedings in the hope that Josie would indeed elongate the conversation to at least the length of the budget section of his meeting. Josie giggled slightly in response before continuing:

"I phoned Steve, as he was the last person to venture into the loft, probably at Christmas when the decorations went back up out of the way. I thought he might have an idea of what might be up there as I haven't been up into the loft in ages. He reckons there is a box or two of old photos and things from when dad went on a tour of Europe with the cricket team. I think he would have preferred Australia or the West Indies but perhaps the team thought they should try and educate our near neighbours instead!"

Josie too was trying to keep the conversation light. "Oh good," replied Colin.

"He also thought there was a small collection of cassettes, that may be from the same time, and he thought that perhaps music would help reposition dad's mind."

Colin felt enthusiastic enough to interject:

"That's funny, as we have just been talking about how music could potentially help in such situations."

"Well, the thing is, we don't have a cassette player anymore. We must have dumped ours when CDs or MP3 players came along. There may be one hiding in the loft somewhere but I wouldn't bet on it. So, do you think you have one anywhere? I know I'm assuming that the tapes will still work but I thought this music idea may be worth a try. What do you think?"

Josie was stuck between trying to be helpful… and potentially looking for an exit from actually being helpful. If Colin remarked that he didn't think the music idea was worthwhile, she could relax in the knowledge that her agony wouldn't be prolonged. If Colin thought the music idea would work, then she could balance her disappointment with being helpful. Colin would hopefully be unaware of her true feelings about her father's demise. Colin was there to try and ease her father's illness to its natural conclusion but in doing so he would invariably lengthen the process. Josie would prefer it if her father didn't wake up one morning. Therein lay the guilt which she was always trying to conceal.

"Oh, good point," responded Colin to Josie's thoughts on needing a cassette player. "I'm not sure if I have one but I'm pretty sure that my mother would. She has loads of old music stashed away – cassettes, 45s and old 78s too! She can't play the 78s anymore but I am pretty sure that we'd have a cassette player lurking somewhere in the house. I'll have a look around. When do you think that you'd be able to retrieve the boxes from the loft?"

"Steve said he'd get up there tonight; he's not busy at work, so he'll probably come home early to do it," replied Josie, again trying to be in helpful mode.

"That would be marvellous! I don't think I'm due to come and see Sam until later in the week but can I pop around before then to pick up whatever you find? I can then perhaps compile something for when I do see your father. If I'm honest, I am not sure if this will work, as your dad and I seemed to lose the connection this morning. At best we'll be able to reconnect; at worst your husband will have got dusty for nothing..."

Josie giggled again at Colin's response before offering her own comments: "Yes, as you know, I'll be here all day but if I do have to go out, I'll phone you."

"Great, see you later!" responded an enthusiastic Colin, who thought he may be getting somewhere at last, and with that he ended the call with the familiar 'goodbye' and the two parted verbal company.

Colin smiled to himself. Having been deflated at his colleagues stealing the limelight from him, he at least now had a positive aspect to continue the day with. And he also had hopefully missed the budget lecture. He therefore gingerly approached the door of the meeting room and entered the domain of fuzzy numbers and boredom. Luckily for him, that aspect had passed and the room was now debating updates on procedures.

"Sorry about that," said Colin, as he took his seat.

His apologies were accepted by a nod in his direction from Tom, who quickly responded with an indication that anything he missed would be e-mailed to him at the end of the day. That brought the team to the Q&A section, which was normally the bit where everybody remained silent so as to end the meeting as soon as possible and to get home.

But Colin hadn't finished his biscuits and he did have some genuine questions that he wanted to put to the floor, so at the risk of upsetting his colleagues he ploughed on with his first question:

"Tom, what are the details that you're getting about the numbers of patients we may be expecting to deal with going forward due to the increase in population around here?"

Tom responded as best he could: "Well Colin, we get regular updates from our colleagues in Housing and their projection for the next ten years is that their coverage will increase by about 60,000 people; that's a net figure taking into account moves away and deaths. Of that 60,000, they estimate that the majority will be young families and professional types taking advantage of the new head offices taking root here, so from our point of view, the net increase in potential cases for our domain is probably quite small. If anything, we may see a reduction as our cases complete and any potential cases move away to quieter environments."

There was an interesting use of terminology: 'cases complete', relating to death of patients, but it was always known that all of their cases would eventually end in death; it was just how long that process would last.

Colin nodded in appreciation of Tom's response and proceeded with a further request:

"So, do we have any plans to protect our position; I mean, if our target market is falling in numbers how safe will we be, as individuals and as a unit?"

For some unknown reason, Colin had been absorbed by business speak but it was a way of making sure that Tom knew of his concerns. Bizarrely, Colin had moved from a happy-go-lucky to serious attendee, but at his age he couldn't afford not to be employed and this was a vocation that he enjoyed.

"I know that you were out of the room when we were discussing the budgets, but we have sign-off for the next five years for our current compliment of staff, so don't worry!"

There was relief on Colin's face as the news was imparted to him. His colleagues already knew their positions were reasonably secure, but most of them were a good ten years younger than him and could afford to change direction. Colin was job-bogged; the job had been so much a part of his life that he didn't have the skills to pull himself out and try some other form of work. He was therefore reliant on the goodwill of his employer. Five years more wouldn't be enough but it would have to do.

"Thanks," he said with genuine appreciation. Tom looked around the room.

"Are there any more questions?"

There was a unified chorus of various forms of the word

'no' and so Tom rounded off the meeting. "Okay people, thanks for your time today and see you all next month; the meeting is set for the 20th again."

The team stood up in unison and started to gather their papers together, whilst making small talk to the people around them. The topics always included the same subjects – football, holidays taken and booked, the weather, and who wants to go for a quick drink? Colin always declined the latter but was always willing to engage on the other subjects. Today he could offer nothing and so he let the others make their plans whilst saying a goodbye to the group. When he thought nobody was looking, he procured the biscuits that had been languishing on his plate. One went into his mouth, which would have precluded him from talking anyway, and the remaining set found their way into his right-hand jacket pocket for later consumption, probably on the drive home.

He was the first to make his way to the lift lobby, leaving the others to arrange where they were going to go for a drink. He wasn't being unfriendly but just had a feeling of foreboding. He couldn't identify why, or what was causing such a feeling, but he just felt as if something was about to change; probably for the worst.

He said goodbye to Cindy on the reception desk and pressed the call button for one of the lifts to appear. There was a short pause before a suitable 'ping' was heard and the doors opened with their customary greeting; whoosh! He turned and smiled towards Cindy, entered the cage and pressed the button marked 'G' that would enable his departure. The whoosh responded to his request and he was soon exiting the building and heading towards his car.

He removed his jacket, whilst carefully juggling with his papers, and reached into his trouser pocket with his available hand, hit the open button on the car key fob, and carefully opened the driver's door with the unused fingers of his right hand. Using his right foot, he held the door ajar whilst lobbing his papers and jacket onto the passenger seat. Having crouched inside and into the driving seat, he carefully searched for his drive home snack and retrieved the saved biscuits, which he placed in the centre tray between the two seats. They wouldn't last for the full journey but they would help.

The drive home was an uneventful affair. The biscuits had basically gone before Colin had pulled out of the car park but he was now home, where there would be a top-up selection for him to graze through should the need arise.

"Hello son," said his mother, as she noticed Colin enter through the front door.

"Hello Mumsie," replied Colin, with his normal tone of relief, which always accompanied him crossing the boundaries of the house. Today however, he was still pestered by a sense of unease. It wasn't an unease that you would normally get before an important football match, but more of an impending situation that wouldn't be pleasant.

"Do you know if we still have a music cassette player?" enquired Colin.

The fact that this was part of the initial opening exchange between them indicated that perhaps his case with Sam was playing on his mind. The connection they had was now likely severed and the route back to a conversation may have been lost for good.

"I think so," replied his mother, "it's probably under the stairs with everything else."

There was a degree of inevitability about the answer. The under stairs cupboard seemed to be a magnet for everything that was too troublesome to do anything else with. The loft was another location where unused or little-used items would spend most of their life, but his mother was pretty sure that a cassette player would be nearer to hand. There were still a couple of unexplored boxes there that Colin hadn't opened yet and doubtless they would contain what he was looking for. Of course, he was banking on the thing actually working, and his fear was that if the player was a battery-operated affair, then hopefully somebody would have taken the old batteries out before putting the item into storage.

"Great! I'll get changed and have a crawl around…again!"

"I'll put the kettle on, then!" responded his mother, as if a trip to the under-stair cupboard was always paired with a cup of tea.

Colin journeyed upstairs to perform his initial task of changing into something more casual whilst his mother carried out her part of the equation. He was soon downstairs again, wearing some slightly less-formal clothes of jeans and an old checked shirt. He proceeded to take up the position required to enter the under-stair cupboard; crouching, kneeling and then a sort of shuffling, as if trying to impersonate Toulouse Lautrec, as he approached the apex of the cavern.

Colin knew which boxes he had seen before and so he started to position and rearrange those to one side, slightly behind him, and he was soon faced with four yet-to-be-visited boxes of various sizes, one of which was the shoe box tied with a bow, which Colin had spied before on his last excursion. The bow implied that this was somehow personal, or more valuable than the others.

Whilst most of the boxes had merely been secured by interlapping the four top flaps, with the exception of his work box that had been sealed with tape, the shoe box was the only one that was potentially special. Colin so wanted to open this box but he was hesitant for fear of something personal to his mother being inside. She hadn't told him not to retrieve that box but she had probably forgotten about it anyway. If Colin asked her whether he could open it and she said 'no', then there would be an even greater temptation to find out what secrets were inside.

He decided to open it and carefully pulled on one of the strands of ribbon to enable the ritual to begin. He tugged a bit harder and the ribbon released its grip on the box lid and the material fell to the sides. The lid was now free to be lifted from its mooring and Colin duly obliged, expecting to see a pair of his mother's dancing shoes inside and, as if to confirm this, he picked up the box again to check the weight before fully pulling off the lid. The weight was reasonably heavy, so a pair of shoes was likely inside. The lid was removed gingerly to reveal, not dancing shoes but what he was actually looking for – a music cassette player, together with some old cassette tapes!

'*Brilliant*', he thought to himself, and he started to rummage through the small collection of tapes, which luckily had been adorned with the actual song titles that had been recorded.

At first, he didn't recognise any of the music, apart from the odd classic that was still popular today, but having been successful in his quest, Colin slowly reversed back out of the cupboard and into the daylight of the hall and living room.

He sat in his chair with a groan, as he hadn't actually managed to get into a fully upright position before collapsing into the comfort of his usual domain. He held the open box on his lap and carefully placed the cassette player on the floor at his feet, and then switched the positions of the box and the player, as he thought it would be more important to check whether the thing was actually operational. He surveyed the player from all angles, looking for any sign of damage and also how the thing actually was powered.

There was the normal array of chunky buttons on the top at the front and at the side was a power connection point. Colin flipped the player over to reveal a battery compartment and he carefully pressed the retaining plate in the direction of a moulded arrow, and with a bit of good luck, the plate moved away to reveal an empty chamber. Luckily the batteries had been removed long ago and the connections looked in reasonable condition for such a piece of old engineering.

Colin swapped positions of the cassette player and the box and luckily found the electrical cable at the bottom, hidden beneath the small library of tapes. He leapt to his feet whilst feeding the cable to the connection on the side of the player and extending it so that the plug was ready for its attachment to today's world.

There was a free socket on the wall to his left and Colin knelt down again to plug the cable into its desired location. He flicked the switch on the wall and gingerly pressed the 'on/off' power toggle on the cassette player. A very welcoming red light illuminated to indicate that all was well. Colin took up the character of Toulouse Lautrec again as he knelt his way back to the box of tapes and retrieved the collection. He then returned them to the cassette player. He picked out the first one he could find and didn't bother to read what was likely to be played. He quickly hit the 'eject' button that propelled the lid of the cassette chamber into an erect position. He placed the cassette inside, closed the lid and pressed hard on the big 'play' button. There was a loud hiss but nothing much else, and so he turned the volume knob down to a reasonable level and awaited something with a tune. But nothing was forthcoming. His slight deflation was interrupted by his mother entering the room with the customary mug of tea in each hand.

"Oh, you've found it," she said, noticing the new position Colin was in. If he wasn't sat in his chair in anticipation of his tea, then he must have been successful in his quest, she thought.

"Yes, but I'm not sure it is working."

"Well, have your tea and have a rest, then see if you can fix it," responded his mother.

Colin duly obliged his mother's suggestion and pressed the big 'stop' button and reasserted his upright stance, whilst walking back to his chair and the comfort of a mug of tea. Tea makes everything feel better.

"I thought I heard it hissing," said his mother, trying to reassure her son, who she could see was not going to get the full benefit of his mug of tea as a result of his adventure under the stairs.

"Yes, it was hissing but there was no music," responded Colin, in a slightly downbeat mode. "Perhaps it needs to be turned over," was the helpful reply.

"Yes, of course! Why didn't I think of that?" and with that expression Colin carefully placed his mug of tea on the floor and sprang to life again in the direction of his new found toy.

He knelt once more and pressed the 'eject' button, which repeated the lid flipping upright and the cassette making itself available for relocation. Colin removed the tape and quickly reinserted it the other way around, pressed down the lid and hit the 'play' button again. This time he had a cacophony of sound; it was music but not something he recognised. It eventually meandered to a chorus which, whilst Colin still couldn't recall what it was, it did resonate with his mother.

Colin had his left side facing his mother and so couldn't see the expression of horror that had permeated her face.

Whilst she wasn't one for wearing a lot of makeup, there was a distinct draining of colour from her face and her eyes became wider with the surprise and shock. This was followed by the build-up of water in her eyes that forced her to squint slightly before her left hand reached up to dry the slight flow. At this point Colin turned around to ask whether she recognised the tune.

"Remember this, Mumsie?" he said, trying to help her with a trip down memory lane. Unfortunately, Colin had chosen the wrong lane as he noticed his mother starting to sob.

"What's wrong?" he exclaimed.

"Turn it off! Turn it off! Throw it away…away I said!"

"Why?! …Why?!" responded Colin, as his mother got up and hurriedly hurtled upstairs towards the sanctuary of somewhere as far away from the music as she could be.

Colin obeyed her instructions and dutifully disconnected the player from its power source and reassembled the items back into the box. The room fell silent.

He needed the cassette player for his work with Sam and so decided to put the box straight into his car. It would be away from his mother and she wouldn't have to see or hear the memories again. But what were the memories that had affected her so? Was it her and his father's favourite song and she had been jolted back to a time when she should have been happy? He didn't ask himself anymore questions and just carried out his best idea of positioning the box in the boot of his car. He opened the front door and completed the task.

Returning to the house and closing the door behind him, he then considered his next move; should he go upstairs to comfort his mother, or should he let her ride out whatever it was that had upset her so much. He dithered before finally placing his right foot on the first step of the stairs.

His earlier unease had been justified.

CHAPTER ELEVEN
Old Memories, New Beginnings

Colin kept to his threat of visiting Josie to pick up the box of memories which Steve had retrieved from the loft. As always, the front door had been left slightly ajar to enable him to access the house with the minimum of hindrance. He had deliberately parked his car away from its normal visible location; this was not a formal visit, and he didn't want Sam to peer out of the window and see his arrival, and therefore be expecting him to journey upstairs for one of their regular potential chats. Any disappointment that Sam may have felt at being omitted from proceedings could have further enhanced their recent severance.

"Hello," said Colin quietly, as he entered through the door frame.

"In here," was whispered back by an unseen voice that invited Colin to enter the front room, which is what he would have done anyway without the instruction.

"We found these," said Josie, volunteering an old shoe box in his direction.

The box was a dull grey colour with a faded sketch of what presumably had originally been inside. It looked like a pair of cricket shoes had been the original occupants, as even the faded image couldn't hide that these were a sturdy pair of men's white, studded laced shoes. Size 10, made in England was also cheerfully detailed on the side.

Colin removed the lid to reveal a few cassette tapes, some photos of distant players in a cricket match and some postcards. From his initial viewing, he would opine that the photos of cricket were taken abroad and were the catalyst for the subsequent postcards. He turned over one of the items to reveal a hand written message declaring how the team had won their opening three matches against the local opposition teams. The postage stamp in the top right corner would confirm that those teams were French, probably somewhere in the south, judging by the postmark that proudly shouted: 'CANNES', in letters larger than the corresponding posting date, which had become smudged.

The writing was neat and legible and not long in detail; more of a brief summary of where the writer was and where they were off to next. If Colin had the time, he could probably line up all the postcards and plot the actual journey route. He picked one of the photos at random. It was a proud photo of the team kneeling and standing in front of a cup; obviously the team had been successful on their continental tour. Colin turned the photo over. On the back in the same writing was a very brief description: 'We won! Me and the boys in Marseilles.'

"These look great!" said Colin, briefly looking up in Josie's direction.

"Yes, we had a quick look ourselves. There's one in there where dad looks absolutely sloshed."

She reached towards the box and had a rummage before retrieving the colour photo of about two dozen teenagers, all far too drunk to know that a photo had even been taken. Colin had initial trouble in identifying Josie's father but eventually focused on the eyes of one of the characters in the foreground. They were dark brown and although they, like the photos, had faded over time, Colin could still match the image in the photo with the decade's older owner languishing upstairs.

"I'm afraid dad liked his drink!" continued Josie.

"Yes, I can see that!" responded Colin, who by now had recovered the box from Josie and was busy rummaging for another opportunity to travel on his own visual European tour. He picked a postcard which just had an image of two steins of beer and a large pretzel. *'Germany'*, he thought. He then focused his attention on the half dozen music cassettes, which were strewn in all corners of the box, probably because he and Josie had both been interfering with the contents.

"I did find my mum's old cassette player," volunteered Colin, as he flipped over a cassette to reveal the contents as the other side was blank. It just said 'Tour Music', and so he assumed that this was to keep the team happy on long coach journeys across various boundaries of Europe. Another had a more detailed description listing all the songs of the era. He recognised some but a lot were too obscure for him.

"Great," said Colin, with a degree of finality, indicating that he should leave, and he put the lid back on the box, hiding the contents away for later in the day. He couldn't help noticing that the male species would just pair the box with its lid, whereas the likes of his mother would additionally tie a bow around the contents, either to add a degree of security to the proceedings, or to identify the item as something special.

"I'll have a good look through and try and put these into

some order for a plan. I may start with the photos and the postcards and see if I can use those to jog your father's memory. I should be able to work out from the postcards how old your dad was. I take it that all the writing is your father's?"

"We think so. It all looks the same, so I guess it must be, although dad did once tell us that he and Uncle Jack both originally had tape players and used to swap cassettes."

"Great," said Colin again, slightly overusing the expression, and he smiled at Josie before making his way to the hall and ultimately the front door.

"Bye!", he whispered.

Josie reciprocated as Colin made his way up the path and turned right, away from the potential gaze of Sam, and proceeded towards his parked car. There was a slight skip in his step as he was genuinely looking forward to trying to engineer a segment of time travel for both him and Sam.

He carefully opened the car door and placed the box of goodies on the passenger seat. He now had the problem of where he was going to peruse the contents. If he only collated the photos and postcards, then he could probably do that at home. The music cassettes would have to be listened to away from his mother, as she was obviously sensitive to music of that era, although he still didn't understand why. Having followed her up the stairs the other day after the fallout, she had refused to talk about the incident and Colin naturally adhered to her request; he was curious but the love for his mother was the greater part of the equation.

Colin inserted the car key into the ignition and started the engine. He reached for the seat belt and plugged it in, signalled to move away and checked the mirrors. In the absence of any formal appointments for the day, he decided to go home and carry out the investigatory work. His alternative was the office, but once there he could be bogged down in office politics, which along with budgets, was not his favourite subject.

His drive home would be a longer route but there would be tea and biscuits there. He therefore turned the car around at the roundabout at the end of the road and proceeded home, slowing down slightly as he passed Josie's house and glancing up to see if Sam was looking out. There was no sign of him, which could mean one of two things; either Sam only looked out of the window when he knew that Colin was due, and he didn't realise that the two of them had recently been in the same house, or he deliberately chose not to look out of the window in protest that Colin was no longer welcome.

Colin's plan for a bit more time travel was resting on the contents of the shoebox and he glanced down at the package, as if praying for its assistance. He had never had a case where he hadn't seen the procedure through to the patient's eventual death, and whilst he had met with brick walls on many occasions, they had never occurred after he had managed to form a connection with the person.

The drive home was uneventful and Colin soon found himself parked on his driveway. His mother was looking through the window with a surprised but happy expression on her face. She had presumably heard a car pull up, and not expecting her son home for some hours yet, she naturally wanted to know who was interrupting her day. Colin was an acceptable visitor. She disappeared from behind the glazing and was soon at the front door, opening both it and her smile in equal amounts.

"This is a nice surprise!" she beamed, "you heard me boil the kettle, didn't you?!"

"Of course," replied Colin, exiting from the car and clutching the shoebox close to his chest.

"I thought I'd do some work from home. I'm not interrupting; you haven't got a meeting of the WI in there, have you?!"

"No, no," responded his mother, turning towards the kitchen to amass the usual tea and biscuits.

Colin closed the door behind him and entered the front room. Rather than sit in his normal comfy chair, he decided to place the box on the small dining table that nestled in the front bay window. The flat surface would enable him to spread out the contents of the shoebox. There was a big enough space in front of his armchair but that would involve him either bending over for long periods, or sitting on the floor and getting cramp. The upright nature of a dining chair would be more suitable, and whilst it didn't matter, it would also look more professional. He could also watch the world go by when he needed inspiration.

The tea and biscuits arrived which prompted Colin to move back to his drinking position; the armchair. "Here you go," said his mother, thrusting a mug and a small plate of biscuits in his direction.

"Thanks Mumsie," said a thankful son.

"What brings you home so early?" enquired his mother.

"Oh, I thought I'd bring some work home. I have a box of old photos and postcards that I want to try and use to help one of my cases; jog their memory with a bit of luck."

"That's nice," responded his mother, who had never really been interested in her son's work. She knew what he did for a living and roughly what it entailed, but as for a detailed conversation, that was beyond her requirements. She had never been one for detail. As long as her son seemed relatively happy, then she would let him get on with his workload. She appreciated that he couldn't discuss specific cases; she wouldn't be interested anyway. There was a defence mechanism that she had, which automatically distanced her from anything she didn't want to know about. The more she knew, the more she would worry about the world, so she kept her life simple and safe.

"Yes, there are some interesting old photos of my client's cricket tour and some corresponding postcards, so I am going to try and align them in some form of order so that I can hopefully cheer the old boy up," said Colin, in a manner that invited a conversation but all his mother could say was:

"That's nice, dear."

Deep down she probably had a fear that she was approaching an age where she could be subjected to the very conditions that her son had to deal with at work. He presumably would know how to care for her if the occasion ever arose, but would it be fair on him to subject a more personal avenue into his life? She hoped she would die quickly, like her late husband, to spare her son any lingering anguish.

"I'll get started after this cuppa," replied Colin, raising his mug, as if trying to enhance his sentence, and took a biscuit from the small plate which he had balanced on his lap.

He deliberately declined to volunteer that the box also contained some music cassette tapes; that subject matter was clearly not to be broadcast to his mother. He would have to play those when he was alone in his car or back at the office. He might not even need to use the tapes if the photos and postcards were sufficient to bring Sam back to life, and the tapes could be kept in reserve for when Sam would inevitably clam up again, when something didn't go quite right in his world. Colin knew from experience how unpredictable these situations could be and all he could do was hope and use that experience to nurture his clients back to some form of order.

He finished his tea and the remaining biscuits, made his way to the kitchen to place his mug in the sink ready for washing, and returned to the front room to begin the task of chronologically arranging the contents of the box. His mother remained seated in her chair, slowly drinking the remnants of her tea.

Colin sat at the dining table and took the lid off of the box, trying desperately not to disturb the cassette tapes, which he was fearful of clattering together, and which would alert his mother to the fact that he had other items, apart from the declared photos and postcards. He therefore slowly removed whatever paper-based objects were easily to hand, arranging the cassette tapes so that they formed a plastic base.

It was a military style operation of stealth and skill, reminiscent of a game of Ker Plunk, where the player had to remove long plastic needles from an upright plastic column, without allowing the marbles cocooned above to fall into the tray below. When he was a small child, he had always wanted his removal attempt to release a torrent of marbles that would clatter forever as they bounced into the tray below, and it was only after several more serious games that he had learnt that the object was to do the opposite. But he still preferred the commotion of glass hitting plastic. Today he had to be an adult.

He therefore arranged the items into two piles; postcards on the left, photos on the right and began the task of trying to arrange the two sets into some form of chronological order. He started with the postcards as there were less of those; eight in total. He could tell by the stamps on the reverse that the general route would be France, Germany and Italy with The Netherlands either first or last, depending on the route taken.

The postmarks confirmed that The Netherlands had been their last country of the tournament, before presumably catching a ferry from nearby Belgium or Northern France back to England. Colin placed the postcards picture side up, so that they formed a line of colour stretching away from him across the table, with the most recent card being nearest to him. He then turned his attention to the more numerous photos; he guessed that there were approximately twenty or so; probably twenty-four, as he seemed to remember that rolls of film came with a twenty-four option back in those times.

He quickly shuffled the pack on the blank space on the table in front of him. Because he knew the route taken, he could departmentalise the photos into their relevant countries of origin. He therefore had about three or four photos matching with a relevant postcard from the same country, and having quickly looked at the writing on the back, concluded that Sam was probably a teenager of few words, as most of the phrases were along the lines of: 'Me and the boys in Amsterdam', or 'Drinking to our victory in Pisa'. The writing was legible and neat and slightly familiar, possibly because Colin's own writing may have been similar when he was the same age.

Satisfied with his work, he placed the completed piles together to form one big stack, which consisted of a postcard and corresponding photos inter-leaved together. He could then go through the pack chronologically for Sam in the hope that he would remember and be transported forward in time nearer to today; probably only by a few years, but enough that he could declare that progress had been made.

He got up from his chair and journeyed over towards a small cupboard behind the door to the front room, which hopefully would contain some rubber bands to secure his workload. He was in luck and soon had the pack restrained and ready to be returned to the cardboard box.

He carefully wedged the cassettes around the stack of cards and photos, so as to minimise on any unnecessary clattering that might alert his mother to the fact that there were some music cassettes also in the box. He didn't want a repeat of a few days ago when she had broken down on hearing some music; the best bet was to keep cassettes and any form of music away from her as much as possible. He consequently placed the lid back on the box and took the package out to his car.

His mother had been in the kitchen preparing lunch, and on hearing the front door open she naturally assumed that her son had been called away and that their afternoon together had ended as soon as it had occurred. She consequently turned around and was pleased to see Colin return to the house.

"Just putting the box in the car so that I don't forget it tomorrow," he exclaimed. "Oh, that's good. I thought you had been called away."

"Nope, here for good now," responded Colin, who followed up his remark with an often-used request: "Any chance of another cuppa?"

CHAPTER TWELVE
A Picture Paints a Thousand Memories

The time arrived for Colin to make his regular journey to see Sam in the hope that he could resurrect their dialogue. He decided to rely initially on the written words that Sam had anointed on the various items in the box, and leave the cassette tapes as a safety net should there be no recognition or help from him. Whilst music had often been relied on to make a connection with someone's past, he felt that Sam's love of cricket might be the best key to unlock the dilemma.

He positioned his car outside the house in his normal parking spot, which would afford Sam a view of his arrival. He reached across the passenger seat to retrieve the shoe box and took the opportunity to glance up in the direction of Sam's bedroom window. There was no Sam.

He carefully held the box under his arm and exited the car, securing it with the normal press of the key fob button, and proceeded down the garden path. Josie had again heard his arrival and had the front door ajar, which enabled Colin to nudge it open, whilst balancing the box and case in theatrical fashion.

"Hiya!" said Josie in a welcoming manner. "Hiya!" mirrored Colin.

"Okay, let's see what I can achieve with this lot," and he nodded his head in the general direction of his armpit, which was securing the box of photos and cards.

"He knows you're coming," said Josie, indicating for Colin to mount the stairs. He duly obliged.

Reaching the top of the stairs and turning towards Sam's bedroom, Colin again knocked on the door using his elbow to announce his arrival into the room.

"Hello Sam," he said, joyously trying to set the tone for the meeting.

Sam didn't respond, so Colin took the opportunity to sit on the stool and placed the box on the floor in front of him. He removed the lid and took out the bound collection of hopeful time travel material. He removed the first batch of country specific items relating to France.

"Hey! I found these the other day," he said cheerfully, and spread the French collection out in a fan formation with a postcard of the Eiffel Tower on top. He placed them in the direction of Sam's view. There was no response, so Colin removed the postcard to reveal the photo of some of the group of cricketers, which included one of Sam in the foreground.

"That's me!" said Sam, "did you get them from Uncle Jack?"

Colin again thought as quickly as he could. Having confessed earlier to buying the blue Ford from Uncle Jack, he decided to declare that they were in the car.

"Yes, they were in the boot of his car that I bought." "Why didn't he keep them?" said Sam sorrowfully.

"Oh, they were under the mat where the spare wheel was. I expect Uncle Jack had been looking for them and assumed that they were lost somewhere rather than in his car," responded

Colin in storyteller mode.

"Have you got anymore?" responded Sam.

Colin laid out the photos of France in a pre-organised order across the bedsheets in front of Sam, who started to move into life as he surveyed the vista in front of him.

"That's Michael," he announced, "we won that match!"

"I think you won every match according to the notes on the back." Colin reached down to prepare the next batch for inspection by Sam.

"That's Michael again!"

It was evident that the photos were from a particular time that Sam could now relate to. There was a degree of joy in his face, which tried desperately hard to hide his normal haunted look, and as each photo was revealed there would be further words of recognition that brought Sam nearer to today.

It looked as though he had moved two or three years nearer to his true existence. He was now probably eighteen or nineteen years old, whilst his face indicated that he was nearer to forty or fifty, as the chiselled lines that had etched his face for so long receded, and the face that he had been trapped in gave way.

This was truly a successful occurrence and one that Colin desperately wanted to share with Josie, but if he stopped the momentum of feeding Sam with new images, he was fearful that the connection would be lost and Sam would revert to his normal shell of an existence. He consequently continued alone with his quest, both men responding to each other's actions. Sam would recognise an image and would respond, and Colin would feed him another, and as a pair they became a self-propelling machine of images and words.

Both became so wrapped up in the excitement that Colin

didn't realise that he had come to the end of the slide show. His hands were now empty of anything new to show Sam. The room fell silent. Colin quickly retrieved the collection from the bed, trying desperately hard not to mix the contents, as he again proceeded to show Sam the images.

"That's Michael again!" blurted out Sam, as the pictures were repeated to him, but after a few more attempts at repetition, Sam suddenly declared:

"I'm tired now."

The strain of time travel had surely taken hold and Colin decided that perhaps there had been too much for Sam to absorb. Like a sponge, he had become saturated to the point of overflow. Colin therefore collected the images and secured them with a rubber band and placed them back in the box. Sam's eyes had now closed and the chiselled lines engraved themselves once again into his face, so Colin quietly got up from his seated position and proceeded downstairs to an expectant Josie, who had naturally heard the activity.

"What happened up there?!" she said, with more expression than Colin had ever seen before in her face.

"It seemed to work!" beamed Colin, who couldn't hide his pride.

"He recognised them?" enquired Josie.

"Yep! Nearly every one that contained him or Michael got an excited acknowledgement," replied Colin, still beaming at his success. He continued with his pride:

"Right, you'd better hang onto these," he said, thrusting the box back in her direction.

"What I'll do is use them again on my next visit. I am mindful that what we achieved up there has truly worn him out and I guess that he is now sleeping off his journey. I'll bring in the cassette player next time, just in case the pictures don't work, that way I'll have a chance of maintaining the momentum. I guess he's eighteen or nineteen…"

"Maybe twenty…I'll have a look at the postmarks," and Josie hurriedly opened the box to flick through to the first postcard, and bending it back she tilted her head to read the date.

"Eighteen," she declared, having done a bit of quick maths in her head. "Great!" said Colin, who still hadn't lost the enthusiasm from his face.

Josie put the box on the side table adjacent to the family portraits and stepped back with a smile. "Okay, see you next time," she declared with a sigh of happiness.

"Yes, hopefully we're making a bit of progress," and with those words of triumph Colin turned and exited into the hall and subsequently out through the front door and up the garden path.

He hit the button on his key fob and the car duly gave him permission to enter. He opened the door, sat triumphantly in the driving seat and glanced up at Sam's bedroom window. Sam wasn't there and Colin surmised that his head was now resting on a pillow and consequently out of sight. He turned the key in the ignition, put his seat belt in place, looked in his mirrors and drove off on what could have been a victory lap.

A good day, he thought.

CHAPTER THIRTEEN
Past Imperfect

Later that week Colin continued the plan to metaphorically hold hands with Sam on his journey. This time he had his music cassette player and some spare batteries, all contained in a cloth shopping bag. As he exited his car, which he had parked in its regular space outside Josie's house, he naturally glanced up towards Sam's bedroom window. He was there and staring out through Colin as if he wasn't there. The gaunt face had returned.

Josie greeted Colin at the door with a smile but which hid some of her more personal feelings. The guilt of not wanting her father to get better had been playing on her mind during the intervening period, and she felt that perhaps she had been temporarily lifted by Colin's own enthusiasm at the success he had had with the postcards and photos.

She too had been carried away by the scenario, but when she was alone all she could think of was that her father was probably six or seven years older than when Colin had first visited. Her father was therefore likely to be a further six or seven years away from departing her world. She didn't have that long left in her to start a family. Her father may have to go into a home and she would have failed him.

"Hi, I've brought the cassette player this time, just in case. And some spare batteries…just in case," said Colin, sounding joyful.

"Oh good," responded Josie, as hopefully as she could manage, as she led Colin into the front room.

"Have you got the box?"

Colin didn't need to ask the question as he could see out of the corner of his eye that the shoebox was where Josie had left it, nestling amongst the family photos. But he did notice that the happy picture of Sam, which had been subjected to a broken glass front, was now resplendent with a new unbroken pane.

"New frame?" enquired Colin, looking at the picture.

"No, just a new piece of glass. I thought as dad was getting better, I should finally make his picture better too," replied Josie, who managed to contain the lie about her feelings.

"Nice. New Sam upstairs… and downstairs!" he remarked, and awaited Josie passing him the box which he added to his cloth bag. He was ready to climb the stairs and continue the time travel routine.

As he knocked and entered the room, he could see that Sam was still staring out of the window. Colin sat down in his regular place and reached inside the cloth bag that he had put on the floor in front of him. He retrieved the box, took off the lid and removed the elastic band from the postcards and photos. He selected the journey through France again and placed the items in front of Sam.

Sam turned his head slowly and glanced down. There was no recognition of the postcard, so Colin removed that from the top of the pile to reveal the photo of him and Michael and the rest of the cricket team enjoying themselves. Again, there was no recognition, and irrespective of which photo Sam was shown, he declined to travel to that place and time, and it was therefore no surprise that some twenty-four photos and eight postcards later, Colin had to resort to music. Eighteen had reverted to probably sixteen.

Colin removed the player from the bottom of the cloth bag. He had inserted new batteries that morning, so all should be well. He selected the most easily accessible cassette and hit the 'eject' button with his other index finger. The cassette flap leapt to attention with a 'ping', which attracted Sam's attention, and he turned his head further around in the general direction of the new sound.

Colin inserted the cassette and closed the flap, hit the 'play' button and waited for whatever sound would be emitted. He glanced at the volume control, which he had set to three on the ten-notch scale, and soon heard the familiar sound of a crackle as the early part of the tape wound through the clever bit of the player. A song started to reveal itself.

Sam looked at Colin as the sound turned into a tune and the tune turned into recognition on Sam's face. Again, the gauntness started to fade and a more youthful expression gained superiority on Sam's face. Colin didn't recognise the tune but he wasn't the important person in the room. There was a slight movement to Sam's right arm as he attempted to match the beat of the music with his own internal rhythm. He was out by about a beat, but when the chorus arrived that enabled him to catch up, and for the rest of the tune he was pretty much in time.

The next tune followed and again Sam started to match his movement with that of the song. Colin thought there was a danger that Sam might finally get out of bed and dance, and that his 'broken leg' would be cured by the music.

Colin now had a dilemma; he had burned through all the photos and postcards in one sitting, and when he revealed them again there was no positive action. He didn't want the same scenario with the music, so he thought that he should allow two more songs to revolve around in Sam's head and then he would leave the rest of that tape for another day.

The second song finished and they both awaited the intervening hiss to make way for another adventure. Another song materialised and this time Colin recognised it, and he too began to jig on his stool as the song built up to the chorus as he mouthed the words in unison with the singer. Sam was only in rhythmic twitching mode and his lips remained together.

So entrenched was Colin, that he didn't notice that Sam's rhythm was losing its pace, and by the end of the third song his energy levels had dropped to that of a child, who is too tired to eat his food and ends up crashing his face down into his spaghetti hoops. The fourth song therefore only had Colin jiggling in time. He didn't know the song but he did recognise enough to partake in its magic. He looked at Sam. He was asleep, and so Colin fumbled for the 'stop' button and hit it with the required force.

Sam briefly opened his eyes, but then quickly shut them, as the party was now over and he could rest. Colin assembled everything into his bag, got up from his seat and quietly exited the room. Again, Josie was waiting for him at the foot of the stairs. Colin could never ascertain whether she was always there, or whether her timing was such that she could always make it to the same position at short notice, probably when she heard an upstairs floorboard creak.

"He's asleep," whispered Colin, as he made his way down the stairs.

"I'm not surprised! It sounded as though you were having a party up there!" she responded. "Well, he certainly recognised the tunes; I even got a bit of movement out of him!" glowed Colin.

"Gosh! That's not happened in ages," said a surprised Josie, who had made way for Colin to pass her, but as she was now blocking the entrance to the front room, Colin assumed that the invite was to continue to the front door and leave. He did, exchanging goodbyes and walking with a slight skip to his car.

He didn't need to turn around to see if Sam was looking out of the window, as he knew he would be asleep and out of view, but habit was such that his muscle memory told him to do so. Sam was absent, and so Colin did the necessary starting procedure for a trip home and manoeuvred his car out into the road and away from the scene of his victorious event.

The drive home was uneventful until he reached a set of traffic lights that were roughly halfway along his intended route. A niggling thought had entered his head. It had probably been there for some time, but it had chosen to come to the fore as Colin waited at the lights whilst he had nothing to do. The last song that Sam had fallen asleep to, which Colin didn't know but which he thought he recognised; he had heard it before, but where?

The lights changed and Colin pulled away slightly more slowly than he should have, as the impatient driver behind reminded him of his duty to other road users by giving a loud toot and a corresponding glare into Colin's rear view mirror. There were also words, but Colin couldn't lip read.

There was a large supermarket on his side of the road and Colin therefore drove the necessary short distance and indicated to turn left. The man behind looked pleased.

Colin found a suitable parking space away from the trollies, that had a mind of their own, and stopped the car. He rummaged in the cloth bag, which he had placed on the passenger seat, retrieved the cassette player and hit 'play'. The song continued its journey and Colin began to carry on where he had left off by anticipating the nature of the tune and where it was going. He eventually recognised it; it was the song that his mother had been so upset by, and just to make sure he got out of the car and opened the boot to retrieve the selection of cassettes that he had hidden there.

He rummaged again, pulled out the one that he thought had caused his mother so much distress, got back into the driver's seat and switched the two cassette tapes. He hit 'play' again. The music that filled the car was at an earlier place than the other cassette, but that made it easier for Colin to repeat his thought process and match the two together.

He was soon at the same place, and he realised that it was indeed the track that his mother had broken down to. Somehow Colin felt her pain again and quickly hit the 'stop' button and then the 'eject' button. He retrieved the offending piece of plastic and looked at it. He wanted to throw it out of the window so that he would never have to hear it again, but as the song was also on Sam's tape, he would have to dispose of both. He picked up the other tape with his free hand. Both were now in view awaiting their fate, but in deciding what to do with them, Colin noticed that the writing seemed to be the same; neatly written in capital letters in a faded black ink. The vowels and most of the consonants looked identical.

It took him about thirty seconds, constantly staring at the objects in his hands, before the frightening thought struck him with such a jolt that he almost vomited. His mother must have been the lodger at the house that he had been visiting…Uncle Jack must have raped her there and that is why she broke down uncontrollably when she heard the music from that era. She associated the music cassette with her rape and Colin had been stupid enough to bring all those memories back, not only into his mother's life, but also into his own. His father was Uncle Jack; he was the son of a rapist.

He couldn't hold his stomach together any longer, and whatever contents were in there were quickly dispatched and hurled onto the dashboard in front of him. He gagged again and the tears that naturally formed on such occasions were quickly accelerated by tears of sadness, and he was now haemorrhaging from several openings at once, all in an uncontrollable manner.

Luckily, he had parked well away from other shoppers and his demise was only witnessed by his own rear-view mirror. He stared at the re-decorated dashboard, that now had a thin film of opaque liquid and indeterminate solid matter dotted at irregular intervals. The vision made him wretch again but there was nothing more to be propelled. He slowly reached into his driver's door side pocket and retrieved a cloth, which he usually used to wipe the inside of the windscreen when it fogged up, and he slowly mopped up the mess that confronted him.

Wiping his mouth with his handkerchief, he collected the remnants from his face, and in an exhausted fashion discarded the soiled pieces of material into the passenger footwell. He was so tired that he couldn't be bothered to find a more permanent place to discard the offending items; they would have to remain there for at least the remainder of his journey home.

He reached into the glove compartment and searched for something cleansing to aid his appearance. Luckily, there was a small packet of moisture wipes that Colin used when he had eaten his lunch on the move and needed to wipe his hands before seeing a client in the afternoon. They served a dual purpose today; they refreshed and cleaned in equal measure, and he was soon looking at his improved image in the mirror. Apart from around his eyes he looked as normal as he could. The dashboard and instrument panel were also given a wipe, and again the soiled remnants were thrust into the footwell on the passenger's side.

As he slowly recovered his composure, Colin realised that he still had the Florida phone number stored in his private phone that would connect him to Sam's own father. He recalled that George had held back on some bits of information, but Colin had to know whether Uncle Jack was the person who had attacked his mother, and by inference, whether he was actually Colin's own father. He had to know whether that bastard's actions had actually resulted in his own bastard status. And he had to hear the words from the family who were responsible. The sound of their own words would secure the truth; what he did with that truth would be the next issue for Colin to resolve.

He glanced at his watch and noted that the time would be about 10am in Florida. He delved into the hidden foothills of his case and retrieved his personal phone. He hurriedly switched on the device and eventually it blossomed into life. The battery level was declaring a likely problem, and so Colin again fumbled in his bag and retrieved the necessary charging cable. He connected the two together and plugged the important end into the cigarette socket, which was confirmed by a satisfying 'beep' and a movement of graphics, which indicated that the device was taking on power.

He carefully retrieved the required phone number from his storage and hit the green phone icon that would connect him with – hopefully - the truth. There was a pause and the unusual ringing tone that indicated he was on target. The ringing tone continued… and continued… and continued, and Colin felt that he would have to abort his quest, but just as he was about to give up there was a helpful response:

"Hello?"

It was a familiar voice, and whilst Colin didn't have to confirm who it was, it was nevertheless protocol to do so.

"George?"

"Yes, who's this?"

"Not sure if you remember me; it's Colin Smith, I'm writing that book about the local area and you kindly helped me out when I phoned a couple of weeks ago."

There was a degree of desperation in his voice, which luckily must have got lost somewhere in the Atlantic, as George did indeed remember.

"Yes. Sorry, was I expecting you to call today?"

That was the awkward question which Colin had to deflect. He had not cleared the call with Josie. And he had not indicated that he would be making any such call, but he was hopeful that George would indeed remember that he had got acceptance to calling again at a later date, should he need to.

"No, sorry but I'm just wrapping up some final points in my book and I hoped you could help. I think you were open to another call."

That was said with a degree of hope. Luckily, there seemed to be little resistance from four thousand miles away.

"Yes, I did, didn't I."

Colin didn't dwell on the slight hesitation in George's reply and ploughed straight on with his required questioning:

"So, I want to just finalise on your brother's character a bit more. I know you said he was a wrong 'un but do I take it that the attack on the lodger was never reported to the Police, as I cannot find any records of a sentence, or even anything in the local court archives."

Colin realised that he hadn't warned George about what he specifically wanted to know. Nor had he actually bothered to research the archives for anything, but George didn't know that, as was evident by his reply.

"You won't. The woman never reported it to the Police… and we certainly weren't going to report it. I paid the woman to keep quiet, and if she hadn't then I don't know how we would have disguised the incident. Anyway, you're not going to print this, are you?"

George had just realised that he was giving too much information and Colin was currently unaware of the slight discrepancy in what he had just heard. But he would recognise it shortly.

"No, it's just so I can put a bit more into the characters of the era. I am not using their actual names where something awkward or sensitive is part of the story. I am just categorising individual types and mentioning names only where it is positive; like erecting of statues or charity events etc."

"No, please don't mention our names," pleaded George.

"I won't. You can have a copy of the draft before I put it to print," responded Colin, who was digging himself into a deeper hole by perpetuating the deceit. But then the discrepancy in George's earlier comments hit him:

"What did you mean... by disguising the incident?"

Colin waited the reply, and it was evident that the flow of the conversation had stuttered at this point, as it was now more of an interrogation. Eventually there was a hesitant response from Florida.

"Look, my brother was the wrong 'un, and he had been in enough trouble with the law, but he was innocent. Sure, he and Sam were drunk that night, and I know he wasn't helpful by not stepping in, but it wasn't him that attacked the woman... it was my son; it was Sam. Please, Josie doesn't need to know this."

Colin remained silent at the consequences of what Sam's father had just divulged. The silence was accompanied by a blast of coldness that permeated every fibre of his body. Somehow it was complimented by a warm sweat that seemed to emerge from his forehead, armpits, groin and neck all at the same time. His body was as confused as his mind and he felt a further gagging building up, which he had to resist and fight against. The silence continued, which prompted a reluctant George to ask whether he was still there:

"Hello? Are you still there?"

Colin fumbled for some form of answer and he had to delve deep into his memory for a response.

"Yes... yes, I think so," was the stuttered reply which was eventually produced from his end of the conversation.

"Sorry, can you run that past me again?" continued Colin, with a slightly more controlled nature to his voice but with a temperature battle still raging inside him. Luckily the threat of vomiting had been nudged out of the way and replaced with an incredulous desire to hear that news again.

"Sam was the one that attacked the woman. He and my brother had been out drinking that night, came home and found the woman alone in the house, and I suppose a mixture of the drink and the opportunity was too much for him to resist. I don't know the full details, I just blamed Jack for not asserting his authority and preventing the incident; he was the oldest. It cost me a couple of hundred quid to keep the woman quiet and we kicked Jack out. I am trusting you not to tell Josie any of this; it would kill her if she knew her father was guilty of raping some poor woman…"

Colin was still experiencing his own internal battle of warm and cold fronts, which were fighting for supremacy within his body, and he couldn't be sure if he had actually heard what George had just said, as he was concentrating on the aspect that Sam had attacked the poor woman. Deep inside the cyclone that was battering through his body, he must have known that the woman was his own mother and that compelled him to ask a pertinent question:

"Do you remember the name of the lodger?" he enquired, hoping somehow that his mother wasn't the lodger at the time, and that another woman had been the victim, either before or after his own mother's stay.

"No, it was a long time ago. Oh wait…it was Smith…Lucy or Lesley, or something beginning like that.

I should remember, it cost me two hundred pounds, which

was a hell of a lot of money back then…"

Colin couldn't help but volunteer the final bit of information that George was seeking as he proudly announced his mother's name:

"…Lilian?"

"Yes, yes, I think that was it…how do you know that?!" responded George, with more than a degree of curiosity in his voice.

Colin had to think quickly to deflect any suspicion of his own family's involvement. Whilst George was a ninety something year-old father four thousand miles away, Colin now realised that his son was now his own father, and that thought resurrected the weather battle within him again. He could only guess at what would be an acceptable reply and from somewhere he conjured up a winning response:

"Oh, we've been looking at names to call our own daughter when she is born, and we rather like the name Lilian."

Somehow that calmed the storm, both inside him, and the one that could have developed in Florida, had the conversation taken a different course. George responded positively and the exchange was taken away from earlier rapes to the joys of a new born.

"Oh, that's nice. That is a nice name; I hope it all goes well for you."

"It will," said Colin, who had now got control of his body and was in a different mood. The shock and disgust of what he had just learnt gave way to something more sinister, and the tone of his words implied that, whilst George had dismissed the event as something that could be bought off, Colin felt that the case was very much still alive.

"You won't use any of that or tell Josie, will you?" were again the pleading words from a man who thought he had escaped his past.

"Of course not," replied Colin, with a chill in his voice that implied that the cold front had won the battle in his own body. "Thank you for your time," he said, looking to finish the exchange, and he hit the red phone icon on his mobile. He didn't know whether George had responded in a similar way, as his desire to end the call and fully digest what he had learnt, was far greater than the quantity of politeness he could attach to the departure.

He sat in his car staring at the dashboard. The strain of trying to hold back his internal emotions whilst hearing the new appalling news, suddenly came to the fore again. Like a dam holding back a trillion cubic metres of water, Colin felt his stomach enter his throat again, and with the smallest of warnings, more indeterminate liquid was projected out of his body and onto whatever static surface was in the way.

Colin reached for the wet wipes again and re-cleaned himself and the dashboard.

Whilst his life was rarely perfect and things didn't always go according to plan, he had normally managed to get through the day without any major shocks. His recent crash, which resulted in him sitting in his current vehicle, was probably the only time something had gone majorly wrong in the last few years. But the news that he now knew who his father was, that he was the result of a rape, and that his mother had obviously been bottling up her feelings for some five decades, meant that this day was monumentally different.

He still felt a whole host of emotions. He was angry that he had been lied to by his mother, angry that she had been raped, angry that he was the direct result of that rape, and angry that he knew that his life was now upside down. Conflictingly, he was sad that he never knew that his father was geographically so close to him, and that he never knew him when he was fit and well and capable of being part of a normal father and son relationship. But most of all he was sad for his mother, whose torment and anguish had been reawakened by him bringing his work home with him. He therefore also felt guilty for hurting his mother again some fifty years after her ordeal. He could never unsee the look of pain in her face whenever her memories had been returned to her. In some ways it would have been best if her own mind had been trapped in an age prior to her being raped, but instead it was his father who was free and back in the past whilst his conquest was trapped and reliving his actions all over again.

In the battle of emotions his love for his mother won. She had been a single mother in difficult times, yet had raised him without any turmoil that he could remember. He felt a duty to her over and above anything else. His work was secondary, and in the moment even his own life was secondary to the love for his mother, but he had to get rid of his anger somehow. He had been on the right track, thinking that Uncle Jack had been his mother's attacker, but Colin had got off at the wrong station, and what had been a difficult exercise in confirming his suspicions, had become something far more complicated and troublesome.

He would have to re-think his life.

CHAPTER FOURTEEN
Hello Old F(r)iend

Another day arrived. It was an important day. Colin would be getting his own car back from the accident repair centre, and it was also his first visit to see Sam since he had learnt that the two of them were genetically connected.

During the intervening period Colin had calmed down and developed an aura that was not within his natural boundary. He was normally a reasonably cheerful fellow, went with the flow and tended not to plan too much. In his mode of employment he never knew how a patient would respond on any particular day, such was their mental state that erratic was considered normal and normal was considered a blessing. Erratic was what he was used to and therefore unplanned flexibility was his modus operandi. But today was different. Today would be a day he had planned for down to every last detail, together with a secondary plan should the situation change mid-flow.

He approached the accident repair centre and noticed that his blue Ford was parked on the forecourt in an easily accessible position. It gleamed in the sunlight, reflecting the sun's emissions from every conceivable surface. It had never looked so splendid.

Colin parked his temporary car as best he could within the

limited available parking area, and having exited the red cage, he meandered over to his own vehicle. He walked around it slowly, squinting at it and surveying the damaged areas that now could not be perceived from the rest of the car.

"What do you think?" said a distant voice, that edged nearer to him as Colin turned around. "It's brilliant! Literally!" responded Colin, who didn't hold back with his compliment.

"Yes, we thought so too," said the voice, "there's some paperwork to sign and you can then just take it away. Have you emptied out the replacement car of anything important?"

"I just need to get my case and cloth bag out. I'm afraid I've left it in a bit of a mess," responded Colin, realising that the passenger footwell probably still contained the residue of his recent adventure into his past.

"Don't worry, we're used to that. It's a temporary car paid for by some big insurance company. Somehow, they always come back thrashed and abused. There should be a support group for them!" chuckled the voice, which Colin now realised belonged to a sturdy guy in overalls that had a pleasant demeanour about him. Colin used to have one of those.

"I'll get my stuff," said Colin.

"Come into the office when you're ready," replied the overalls.

Colin went over to the red car, which had been his mobile office for the last few weeks, opened the driver's door, reached over to retrieve his case and pulled the lever that released the boot. He also decided to insert the key into the ignition to enable the front windows to be lowered. He didn't know how long his car would remain untouched in the sunshine, and he felt obliged to minimise the build-up of any obnoxious smells that might multiply in the enclosed heat.

He pulled out the key once it had achieved the task, and he went to the rear of the car to pick up the cloth bag which contained the photos, postcards, cassette tapes, and the player that would play such an important part in his day. He reached up and pulled down on the hatch and made his way to the office that was situated at the far corner of the parking lot.

"Okay, I've got my stuff," volunteered Colin to the guy, who was now behind a well-used counter and preparing the paperwork for Colin to sign.

Colin slid the keys over the counter and the guy mirrored his action by gently pushing the paperwork in the opposite direction.

"If you could sign where the pencil crosses are, to confirm that you are happy with the repair, I'll let you have the keys and you can be on your way. I take it you've had a good look."

"Yes, it looks fine," responded Colin, not sure if he should take a further look but decided that the work seemed professional enough to warrant his signature where it was needed.

"There you go," and his keys were slid across the counter to Colin's eagerly awaiting hand. "Cheers!" said Colin, and he turned around and ventured towards his gleaming blue chariot.

He hit the necessary button on the key fob and there was the familiar sound of the car's approval. It was like greeting an old friend and Colin opened the door to reveal an equally clean inside. There was a plastic hood, that covered the driver's seat, and a corresponding paper mat in each of the front footwells.

Colin didn't have time or the demeanour to feel guilty about the disparity between his own car and the temporary one that he had been provided with. He placed his case and cloth bag on the passenger seat. He removed the plastic cover and placed it into the passenger footwell, where most discarded things would spend a portion of their life, sat into the driver's seat and inserted the key into the ignition and started the engine.

It purred into life, and Colin realised in an instant how ropey insurance company provided replacement cars were, as this engine sang to him, whereas his recent encounter had a tone of grumbling into life, almost protesting at being asked to do something. Colin put on his seatbelt and looked around him before engaging gear, releasing the handbrake and entering into the road, which was surprisingly clear, giving Colin the impression that his smart new car was worthy of 'Zil lane' status.

He was on his way. He had a date with destiny; Sam's destiny.

The journey from the accident repair centre to his appointment with Sam was an uneventful one, and Colin breathed in the ambiance of his faithful blue Ford. The controls had easily been re-introduced to him, as if they had never been separated. He felt more at home, like slipping on a pair of nicely fitting shoes whose internal dimensions had an agreeable fit with its contents. When he drove this car he didn't have to think about what he was doing; he didn't have to try and remember whether the indicator stalk was on the left or right, he just naturally knew where everything was, and this meant he had more time to consider his future actions.

He pulled up to a stop outside Josie's house and positioned the car in his normal space. He tried the often-used tactic of pretending to retrieve something from the passenger footwell, which provided him with the opportunity to glance up to see if

Sam was looking in his direction. He was.

Colin smiled to himself as he mentally ticked the first box on his 'to do' list. He consequently removed the car key, got out of the car with the two bags secured in his left hand. He hit the lock button on the key fob and this was accompanied by the familiar sound that his car was now secure.

He continued on his journey down the front garden path and for once took in the vista of the well- stocked flower beds, which had a degree of chaos in the blending of their colours, but which at the same time provided an attractive overall image. Colin had no idea which flowers were presenting themselves, and he couldn't make out whether the whole picture had been planned, or whether the garden was the result of a chaos theory approach, where whatever colours emerged had been down to fate and the inability of the owners to distinguish between a weed and a proper flower.

He recalled an answer he had heard to a pertinent question: What was a weed? Basically, anything growing where you didn't want it to grow.

The front door, as always, was ajar and volunteering Colin an easy access to today's major task. "Morning," said Josie, with a cheerful smile accompanying her words.

"Morning," responded Colin, with a smile that he hoped mirrored hers but which may have been a bit too false had she noticed it.

"How's our man today?" continued Colin, trying hard to maintain a degree of normality. "He seems good; a little more alert than usual. I think your process may have worked a bit."

This time it was Josie who was perhaps smiling too falsely as she tried to conjure up words that would imply that she was happy with her father's progress.

"Good, I'll see if I can get another result today," replied Colin, who said one thing and secretly meant another, and he ventured upstairs to continue his work.

He knocked on the bedroom door and entered the room. He could see that Sam was still looking out of the window towards his parked car, but even from the angle he was presented with, he could see that Sam had a slightly puzzled look about him. A normal person probably wouldn't have noticed any difference but Colin picked up the slightest of additional lines on Sam's face.

"Uncle Jack you are back after all! I knew you would come back! Your blue Ford is there!"

The words that were offered with such force by Sam were not in the day's script that Colin had prepared. But as Colin was the only person who had read the script, it wasn't a surprise that everybody else was in the dark. With a slightly hesitant response, Colin replied as clinically as he could:

"Yes, I've come back."

The words were a natural continuation of the conversation, but the problem that was racing through Colin's mind was whether Sam was associating his blue car with a time prior to his late teens, and therefore whether Sam had reverted to an earlier time in his life. Would the contents of the cloth bag be of no use to Colin if Sam hadn't experienced them yet?

"But I thought you'd got rid of it and now had the red one," was the follow up remark that Sam volunteered.

Colin thought he'd try and bulldoze his way through that situation and try and get the conversation back in line with his prepared script. His words were carefully chosen…

"How old are you Sam?"

"Sixteen. You know that!" was the reply that Colin hadn't wanted to hear, and which meant that he may have to freestyle the rest of his time with Sam.

The best he could do was to try and let this part of the conversation fizzle out, so that he could introduce the music cassettes back into any break in the conversation, and therefore try and get Sam travelling in time again to the era that he wanted.

"I like blue cars," confirmed Sam.

"Yes, I know. I like them too, that's why I've got one. Would you like to go for a ride in it one day?" volunteered Colin, taking the conversation beyond his remit.

"Yes!" said a vaguely excited Sam, whose response had erased the additional lines from his face. "Okay, maybe we can go next week. I'll ask your mother if we can do that," said Colin, hoping to bring an end to the blue car topic.

"I've got some photos to show you," continued Colin, as he leant down into his bag to retrieve the box of items that would hopefully bring Sam back on track.

He positioned the postcards and photos taken in France in front of Sam's field of vision, hoping that they would jolt Sam forward a couple of years, but Sam's face just returned to his normal blank, gaunt stare. Colin continued to bring more photos into the realm of possible recollection but each image resulted in just a continuation of disappointment. The pictures of him and Michael, that had produced a breakthrough on a previous occasion, were left languishing as just coloured blurs of nothingness. Adventures in Germany, Italy & Holland, and wherever else Sam had travelled to, were not of importance to him anymore, and Colin concluded that Sam was now stuck too far back in time to be brought forward. He consequently had no option but to dispense with the support act and bring the main feature to the fore in the hope that Sam would be coerced into recollecting his past.

Colin retrieved the cassette player and picked a music cassette that was near its starting point, flicked the 'eject' button to reveal the inner chamber and inserted the item. He closed the flap and pushed the 'power' button. He then hit the 'play' button. There was a slight hiss, indicating that the tape was at a point between songs, but shortly afterwards a series of musical notes were emitted, closely followed by some words.

Colin didn't recognise the tune and neither did Sam, as there was no sign of life from his fingers, that Colin had hoped would start to jig in time with the music. The track continued on its journey through apathetic appreciation and was eventually replaced by a track that Colin did recognise, but which he had no idea who the artist was. He started to mouth the words to himself, replacing those he didn't know with a general movement of his lips that were at least in time with the beat being transferred to his ears. That song ended without any recognition from Sam and Colin began to realise that he may have reached an impasse. He decided to let the tape continue with another track. His desire to win this battle would have to be greater than Sam's stubbornness of refusing to travel in time.

The tape eventually ended and Colin went through the normal procedure of removing the cassette and looking for another. He placed the replacement into its rightful place, closed the flap and hit the 'play' button again.

The tape must have been the one that he had played on the

previous occasion, as it started mid-song and was recognised by him. It was also recognised by Sam, who had started to tap in miniscule fashion; his right forefinger moved in time with the music and Colin breathed a sigh of relief at the first sign of progress. The music continued through to the end of the song and another followed, which Sam again reacted to.

Eventually that tape ended, and Colin quickly immersed himself in flipping the tape over to continue the momentum, but in-between bouts of music, Colin asked Sam a question:

"How old are you, Sam?"

"Eighteen. But you know that," declared Sam.

The music started up again. It didn't matter if Colin recognised the sounds or not. If Sam knew the music and responded to it, then Colin would have ticked another box on his 'to do' list. Sam tapped along.

Eventually a song did play which Colin recognised. It was that song again; the one his mother had broken down to. It must have been a favourite as it was on both sides of the tape and also in his mother's collection. Sam again was tapping along but this time with a bit more vigour, as both his forefingers were in motion.

"Do you recognise this song?" asked Colin.

"Yes, this was the one I first shagged to," volunteered Sam.

Colin's hunch, that the track had been instrumental in his mother's pain, was correct, and he felt a cold wave of hurt permeate his own body, as if in solidarity with his mother. Colin metaphorically ticked another box, and he hesitated before finally plucking up courage to ask a potential checkmate question:

"Who was that with, then?"

"Oh, some tart called Lilian," concluded Sam, in a slightly proud voice.

Colin now had all but two of his boxes ticked. He had not anticipated that Sam would confess his actions to him. Colin had enough evidence from his new grandfather's own lips, and that would have sufficed, but to get the confession from his own father's mouth was an added bonus. The truly sad part was that there was no guilt or remorse being declared by his new father. He had dismissed his mother like a discarded item; she was just a tart to be used and abused.

The rage started to build inside Colin at the injustice of it all, so much so that he hadn't noticed that the tape had moved through another two songs and was nearing the end. So was Sam, as he had now exhausted himself and moved into sleep mode. Colin quickly switched the tapes so that another batch of music would play. Sam stirred slightly but remained in the land of rest. Colin ticked the penultimate box.

He waited whilst the tape played on and just stared at his father peacefully sleeping. His father would be unaware of his crime and the hurt that he had caused, and whilst the real cherry on top of the cake would be an apology of some form, and the recognition that he was the father of a man who was nearly three times his age, Colin knew that he had almost achieved what he had set out to do. He slowly got up from his stool and carefully walked around to the other side of the bed to retrieve one of the spare pillows that was resting on the unused portion of the bed.

The song that had been playing faded to a stop and Colin thought it wise to do the same, so as to not indicate any possible movement to Josie downstairs.

Another piece of music started, and he continued on his quest, returning to his normal side of the bed with his new friend in his hand. He reached the required location in the room and stood in-between the stool and the bed, and began to think through what had happened to him over the last few days… and what had happened to his mother during a likely half an hour ordeal fifty odd years ago.

The rage started to build inside him as the hot and cold fronts again took up their positions within him. His father had been dead to him from birth and now Colin just had to complete that fact. Colin pressed the pillow down hard onto Sam's face, making sure that the pressure was so great that no air could escape nor enter under his revenged grasp. There was a slight twitch from Sam's body, as an automatic body reflex kicked in. Sam's unconscious state may have thought that he had all the energy and strength of an eighteen year old, but his body had departed that era long ago and his seventy-something shell was no match for Colin's downward pressure.

The seconds ticked by and Colin glanced down at the whirling wheels of the cassette tape, just to make sure that there was at least one more song to cover his actions. He let it roll through its pre-determined procedure as the last tune played, and with each drum beat Colin felt his pressure increase in time to the music. His kind eyes were kind no more; they had retreated and been replaced by something far darker, something that had never been awoken before but which had obviously had five decades to mature and fester. The natural rhythm he applied was likely the same rhythm that was the catalyst that brought him into the world. A perverse justice was being served.

The music finally stopped, and Colin slowly released his grip in stages that would have allowed him to reapply the pressure of rage at any point during the removal process. But Sam was truly dead and of no concern to him now.

Colin was now upright and the crumpled pillow remained gripped in his two hands. He leant over his father's corpse and replaced the pillow as near to its original position as he could. He then sat down on the stool and collected together all the items that had been so helpful to him. They were now returned to the cloth bag, never to be needed again. He stood up, and so as not to arouse any suspicion should Josie be listening, said a formal and final goodbye:

"Good bye Sam," he said, with eyes that were now showing signs of relief. The kindness had returned and the manic moments had subsided, hopefully never to be aroused again. He was now in a presentable state.

Josie, as usual, was waiting downstairs and quizzed her guest:

"That sounded as though it went well!"

"Oh, it did," volunteered Colin, with a tone to his voice that had never been heard before.

"...I think I got somewhere today. Most satisfactory," continued Colin, maintaining the sinister tone which Josie had hopefully not picked up on.

"He's asleep again. The music tends to exhaust him, so I should let him sleep it off," concluded Colin, as he positioned himself to face the front door and exit the day's work.

"Oh good," responded Josie, "see you next time!"

"Yes, I'll see you next time," said Colin, putting the slightest of emphasis on the mid part of the sentence.

Colin opened the door and walked slowly up the garden path to where his car was waiting. It must have been his imagination but the flowers looked even more beautiful than when he had arrived. The birds seemed to be tweeting even more than they normally did and Colin felt good. All the boxes had been ticked.

As he approached the driver's door, he glanced up at Sam's bedroom window with a final defiant stare. He opened the door, sat down and placed his possessions on the passenger seat. Turning the key in the ignition and putting on his seatbelt, he checked his mirrors before entering the driving portion of the road. Luckily, he didn't have any more appointments today and so it would be a free afternoon for him; a free afternoon for a man now free of his past.

CHAPTER FIFTEEN
Past, I'm Perfect

Colin's phone played the generic ringtone which he had assigned to clients who were entitled to his mobile phone number. It could have been anyone of three dozen or so households who had the pleasure of his company and who always seemed grateful every time he had visited them. He often thought about differentiating them, so that he could distinguish between current clients and previous ones, where his work had been done and the cases had passed away. It would have made sense to know who was calling for a friendly chat and who was phoning with a problem. He could then decide who to answer before trying to locate his phone, which invariably was across the other side of the room when he was sitting in his comfy chair. However, he knew who was trying to contact him and why they were doing so. It would be Josie and it would be about Sam passing away in his sleep. Luckily, he was sitting in his comfy armchair and had his phone in his hand, as if anticipating the call's arrival.

"Hello," he said, after he had pressed the green icon on the phone's screen. "Hello, Colin? It's Josie."

"Hello Josie," replied Colin, with a degree of calmness that verged on being sinister. "It's dad, he passed away in his sleep this afternoon."

There was a huge amount of emotion in her voice but there was also a battle raging within her that made her words appear disjointed, almost stuttering but without actually interrupting the flow of the sentence.

"I found him asleep when I went to give him his medicine but he didn't respond at all. He's finally gone!"

The word 'gone' had to be guessed at by Colin, as that was the point at which the battle containment was lost and the raw emotion flooded across the network. It was evident that the guilt and sadness of her father's passing was conflicting with the relief and joy of her finally being a free daughter. She knew this day would come, and she was genuinely hoping that it would happen, but now that it was here her remorse had outweighed everything else. She had wished her father dead and The Universe had carried out that wish for her.

"Well, we knew it was going to happen but at least we can believe that your father's suffering has ended and he has gone to a better place," responded Colin, with words that he had used many times before when such situations had occurred. The words may have appeared cold as there was little emotion in his voice, and again they verged on being sinister in their delivery.

"I know, I know," gasped Josie, who was mid-sob.

Colin felt obliged to talk to allow Josie time to recover and become normal again.

"There are various things that Steve will have to do with you; a doctor's death certificate being the first instance, but if there's anything I can do to help, then please let me know. Have you contacted Steve?"

"Yes, he's on his way back from work. I'll have to phone his dad in America too; he should be told. I am also expecting the doctor shortly – oh! I think he is here already. Sorry, I'll have to go."

"Okay. I am sorry," concluded Colin.

The call ended and those last three words were perhaps the most worrying. They were again cold and said in a manner that could mean two different things. There was no inflection in the voice that would indicate any emotion or the true meaning behind them. It was if they were just three typed words alone on an otherwise blank A4 page.

"Sorry for what, dear?" said his mother entering the room.

"Nothing mother, but I feel now that I'm perfect," said Colin, with a degree of hidden satisfaction in his voice.

"Of course, you are," responded his mother, neither understanding why nor bothering to enquire of her son's new status.

"Any chance of a cuppa?"

www.ingramcontent.com/pod-product-compliance
Lightning Source LLC
Chambersburg PA
CBHW071622080526
44588CB00010B/1236